# Praise for
## *Prodependen*

"Removing codependence from the list of diseases that afflict humankind and seeing the cause as a response to overwhelming life conditions rehumanizes those who suffer—both addicts and those who love them. This approach rightly acknowledges them as co-participants in the human journey rather than objects of analysis and treatment. In *Prodependence*, Robert Weiss has not only created a new term but has also boldly challenged the cultural practice of negatively labeling those in service to others. He shows that by doing so, we devalue their selfless efforts and amplify their suffering. This groundbreaking book is a call to awaken from the old way of thinking to find new and positive methods. We recommend it to all mental health providers and to those whose mental health will improve by reading it."

—**Harville Hendrix, PhD**, and **Helen LaKelly Hunt, PhD**,
coauthors of *Getting the Love You Want*
and *The Space Between*

"At last, a therapist who understands the power of love. Bravo, Robert Weiss! Rather than judging the caregivers of addicts as codependents with pathologies of their own, Weiss recognizes them as normal, mentally healthy men and women with a deep and unconditional love for their addicted partner or family member. He celebrates emotional dependence, offering nonjudgmental support and guidance for navigating the difficult landscape of relationship with an addict. By coming from a positive perspective, his concepts offer hope instead of despair for those living in crisis. And as a bonus, it's a fascinating read about the evolution of the recovery movement, and the importance of human kindness and connection in healing."

—**Helen Fisher, PhD**, bestselling author of
*Why We Love, Anatomy of Love*, and
*Why Him? Why Her?*

"Rob Weiss is a clinical pioneer and innovator. In *Prodependence*, he takes issue with the codependence model and replaces it with an attachment-based perspective that is less pathologizing and stigmatizing of an individual or a family's love for an addicted relative. Weiss' work and speculation based on his clinical experience moves the field forward and provides clinicians who work with addictions a lot of "food for thought."

—**Christine A. Courtois, PhD, ABPP**, author of
*Healing the Incest Wound* and *Treating Complex Traumatic
Stress Disorders* (co-authored with Dr. Julian Ford)

"*Prodependence* provides a refreshing, empathetic, and practical approach to understanding partners and families of addicts, and how best to help them learn how to handle their difficult situation. Avoiding the classic split between the trauma and codependency models, Weiss uses the framework of *attachment theory* to avoid blaming or pathologizing their behavior. Instead, he validates and reframes their efforts and provides techniques to help them heal, improve their self-care, set appropriate boundaries for their own behavior, and deal with their challenges. This beautifully written book is must-reading for all those who love an addict, as well as all mental health professionals."

—**Jennifer Schneider, MD**,
author of *Back from Betrayal: Recovering
from the Trauma of Infidelity*

# Other Books by Robert Weiss, PhD, LCSW

*Cybersex Exposed: Simple Fantasy or Obsession?* (co-authored with Jennifer Schneider, MD, PhD)

*Always Turned On: Sex Addiction in the Digital Age* (co-authored with Jennifer Schneider, MD, PhD)

*Cruise Control: Understanding Sex Addiction in Gay Men*

*Untangling the Web: Sex, Porn, and Fantasy Obsession in the Internet Age* (co-authored with Jennifer Schneider, MD, PhD)

*Closer Together, Further Apart: The Effect of Technology and the Internet on Parenting, Work, and Relationships Age* (co-authored with Jennifer Schneider, MD, PhD)

*Sex Addiction 101: A Basic Guide to Healing from Sex, Porn, and Love Addiction*

*Sex Addiction 101: The Workbook*

*Out of the Doghouse: A Step-by-Step Relationship-Saving Guide for Men Caught Cheating*

*Out of the Doghouse for Christian Men: A Redemptive Guide for Men Caught Cheating* (co-authored with Marnie Ferree, LMFT, CSAT)

*Practicing Prodependence: The Clinical Alternative to Codependency Treatment* (co-authored with Kim Buck, PhD, LPC)

# PRODEPENDENCE
### Revised Edition

## Beyond the Myth of
## Codependency

## Robert Weiss, PhD, LCSW

Health Communications, Inc.
Boca Raton, Florida

*www.hcibooks.com*

**Library of Congress Cataloging-in-Publication Data
is available through the Library of Congress**

© 2022 Robert Weiss

ISBN-13: 978-07573-2440-6 (Paperback)
ISBN-10: 07573-2440-1 (Paperback)
ISBN-13: 978-07573-2441-3 (Epub)
ISBN-10: 07573-2441-X (Epub)

Publisher: Health Communications, Inc.
        301 Crawford Blvd., Suite 200
        Boca Raton, FL 33432-1653

*Cover design by Jim Pollard*
*Interior design by Lawna Patterson Oldfield, formatting by Larissa Hise Henoch*

This book is dedicated to the memory of my mother, Elizabeth Weiss, a woman who struggled all her life (and mine) with profound bipolar disorder, unrelenting narcissism, paranoia, and psychosis. She was a brilliant mind, but also one too deeply scarred by mental illness for her to ever reach her potential as a woman, as a thinker, and as a mother. Perhaps due to her deficits, she was my greatest and longest-running prodependence teacher. This is true despite forty-five years of illness, hospitals, emergency rooms, abuse, detachment, enabling, caregiving, rescuing, and broken promises on both sides. This is true despite our many related emotional struggles, some of which still haunt me to this day. And this is true despite all the needed therapy, personal growth, addictions, and losses stemming from that deeply flawed mother/son relationship.

You see, no matter what any therapist, support group or anyone else ever reflected to me, that troubled woman will always be my mom. And I, her son. And within that structure, we both did our broken best to love one another through to the end. Thus I'm grateful to have been the one whispering words of peace to her in her last moments. Sadly, due to mental illness, my mother lacked both the tools and the resilience to thrive and enjoy her life (and those of her children). And yet, despite all her deficits and challenges, this woman managed to offer me just enough to be able to survive until I could find my own path to move from surviving to thriving. Thank you, Mom. This one's for you.

# Contents

Acknowledgments   xi

Preface   xiii

Chapter One  **CARING FOR THOSE WE LOVE**   1

Chapter Two  **INTRODUCING PRODEPENDENCE**   15

Chapter Three  **THE ORIGINS OF CODEPENDENCY**   31

Chapter Four  **THE PROBLEM WITH CODEPENDENCY**   45

Chapter Five  **OUR NEED TO CONNECT**   69

Chapter Six  **ADDICTION IS AN INTIMACY DISORDER**   85

Chapter Seven  **PRODEPENDENCE IN ACTION**   99

Chapter Eight  **PRODEPENDENT RELATIONSHIPS**   131

Definitions and FAQs   149

Endnotes   159

Index   169

About the Author   175

# Acknowledgments

Prodependence is a new concept, but there are many people whose ideas, beliefs, and personal and professional support led to the writing and release of this book. In recognition of this, I wish to acknowledge the following individuals:

- First and foremost, love and thanks to my husband of twenty-plus years, Jonathan Michael Westerman, who is my rock and personal guide to all things prodependent.

- Claudia Black, Melody Beattie, Pia Mellody, Robin Norwood, and all the other progenitors of the codependency field. My deep thanks to you for helping so many people and for laying out a strong-enough path for me to humbly follow in your footsteps.

- Dr. Carol Clark, Charlie Risien, Keith Arnold, Cheryl Brown, Karen Brownd, Dr. David Fawcett (and anyone that I sadly forgot to mention). Thank you for your help with this book (and your involvement in my PhD). You've helped "Dr. Rob" become a reality. And I never saw that coming!

- My work team: Scott Brassart, Stuart Leviton, Karen Brownd, Dr. David Fawcett, and Tami VerHelst. Where would I be without you? I am forever grateful for your teaching me how real support feels. Thank you one and all.

- HCI books. For your encouragement and brilliant insights, especially my amazing editor Christine Belleris and CEO Christian Blonshine.

Lastly and most importantly, as a psychotherapist and author, my thanks to the thousands of addicts and those who love them who have shared their pain, their triumphs, and lives with me throughout the many decades of my own recovery and clinical care. My commitment to you here—as always—is to reduce the stigma of addiction while offering a kinder, strength-based path toward healing.

# Preface

*This Abstract, which I now publish,*
*must necessarily be imperfect ... and I must trust*
*to the reader reposing some confidence in my accuracy.*
*No doubt errors will have crept in, though I hope*
*I have always been cautious in trusting to good authorities alone.*
*I can here give only the general conclusions at which I have*
*arrived, with a few facts in illustration, but which, I hope,*
*in most cases will suffice. No one can feel more sensible than*
*I do of the necessity of hereafter publishing in detail all the facts,*
*with references, on which my conclusions have been grounded;*
*and I hope in a future work to do this.*[1]

—Charles Darwin, *The Origin of Species*

In 1909, Charles Darwin published his now-acknowledged masterwork, *The Origin of Species,* with an introduction (excerpted above) stating that his book was, more than anything else, his opinion, with that opinion based primarily on his experience and observations as a naturalist, geologist, and biologist. He hoped that his theories would be received and investigated by other scientists with an open mind. At the same time, he knew that his ideas were likely to be met with resistance on many fronts.

And that is what came to pass. Even today, more than a century later, with endless research supporting the theory of evolution, *The Origin of Species* is viewed as blasphemy by a significant segment of the world's population. That said, I suspect that if Darwin were alive today to witness the still-ongoing creationism versus evolution debate, he would not in any way regret the publication of his work. I think he might say, "If we do not push forth and test new theories, we do not learn and grow."

With the publication of *Prodependence: Beyond the Myth of Codependency,* I find myself in a similar circumstance—pushing forth a strong opinion based on preliminary investigation, my personal experience and observations as a seasoned addiction therapist. As with *The Origin of Species, Prodependence* draws on a considerable amount of existing research; however, it is not a research-based or research-driven book. Rather, this book reflects my evolving views and opinions regarding addiction treatment, sourced in research, along with personal and clinical experience. No more, no less. Moreover, like Darwin, I fully expect that plenty of people will disagree with what I have to say and what I believe. That's the nature of the beast.

When my colleague and early mentor Patrick Carnes published *Out of the Shadows,* the first book on sexual addiction, a few people embraced his theories, but plenty of others attacked him. The same was true with the beginnings of the trauma movement, humanistic psychotherapy, and lots of other interesting and occasionally brilliant ideas. Some people embraced these new ideas, tested them, and, if the research turned out as hypothesized, validated them, others did not, choosing to cling to old ideas even if those ideas were outdated and not useful.

But here's the deal: If no one risks new ideas, we stagnate rather than progress. I truly believe that. I also understand that leading with new ideas, especially ideas that may disrupt existing norms, is to risk ridicule, derision, and disdain. So, with this book I take an informed risk. That said, I hope you will read what I have to say with an open mind, understanding that it was written with a focus toward improving how we treat and support one another. The goal of this work is not to attack ideas put forth by people who were writing in a different time, but rather to question and broaden them to meet the needs of our current work.

I sincerely hope that some readers will be interested enough in the concept of prodependence to conduct the necessary research that will prove my theories either correct or incorrect. Perhaps, over time, the risk I take here will be rewarded by our learning to better serve those we are tasked to treat—or maybe not. The ideas are here; their proofs lie ahead.

Note: I have focused this book primarily toward addicts and loved ones of addicts because those are the populations I have worked with for nearly thirty years, and the people I believe to be most in need of a new treatment method. I nonetheless believe the tenets of prodependence as discussed in this text, rooted as they are in attachment theory and interdependence are sound when extended to any type of mutually dependent relationship. Thus, it is my hope that prodependence will resonate and encourage all readers to remain healthfully committed to looking out for (and hanging in there with) those they love—especially when times get tough.

I am not certain that everything I've written in these pages is as accurate, succinct, clear, and useful as I would like. In truth, I began working on this project several years ago, and even as I write this preface, my theories and ideas are evolving. Thus, I will no doubt find myself looking back at this text in a year or two and saying things such as, "Wow, I wish I'd stated that sentence/idea/example/ concept differently."

So be it.

I recognize and accept that this book will not be perfect or even a fully finished product. And that is okay because my goal here is not to dazzle but to spark interest, discussion, analysis, experimentation, and, hopefully, in time, a modicum of much needed psychotherapeutic progress. My sole aim is to push the addiction treatment field (and perhaps psychotherapy as a whole) forward a step by focusing less on an individual or family system's brokenness and more on the inherent strengths of human attachments.

## Chapter One

# CARING FOR THOSE WE LOVE

*The people we love are the foundation of our lives.*

—Robert Weiss, *author*

## RIDDLE ME THIS

If my beloved wife of twelve years received a cancer diagnosis and we had two kids under the age of seven, would anyone judge me for doing everything possible—even to the point of giving up important parts of my life—to keep my family stable, safe and relatively happy? If I took on two jobs, quit my exercise program, resigned from the company softball team, gained weight and stopped seeing friends to address this unexpected family crisis, would anyone in my life call me out as *enmeshed or enabling?* And if I went to a support group for families of cancer patients, would they ask me to explore the ways in which my dysfunctional childhood might be pushing me into an "unhealthy obsession" with my wife's cancer diagnosis?

Of course not.

To push this example a bit further, what if my wife refused to accept the traditional medical route to healing, deciding instead to rely on unproven herbal treatments? In that situation, should I support my wife's attempts to heal "her own way" even if I disagree? Should I spend every waking moment trying to convince her to trust Western medicine? Should I try to slip prescribed but unwanted medications into her tea when she's not looking? And if I did any or all those things, would the people in my life think of me as overreactive and enmeshed? Would they think that my dramatic refocus away from my goals to help my family was a negative manifestation of my traumatic past? Or would they have empathy and compassion for my grief and unshakable commitment to those I love?

To be honest, I have no idea how I would act under those circumstances. I might make the right decisions. I might make the wrong ones. Either way, I know that I would be doing the very best I could to help my spouse heal and to care for my children. And I wouldn't let anyone—friends, family, my employer, a member of the clergy, my therapist, or anyone else—tell me that my attempts to help were borne out of anything but healthy love and attachment.

Of course, nobody in my world would try to tell me otherwise in this situation. Instead, friends and family would show up on my doorstep with flowers, home-cooked meals, and offers to help with childcare, shopping, yard work, and housecleaning. Meanwhile, my therapist, clergy, and employer would understand and accept that my family is in crisis, I love them, and that right now I must give of myself in an extraordinary way, even if that looks a little obsessed or makes me seem a bit nutty at times. And if any of these supportive individuals felt that I was overdoing my attempts at caregiving, possibly to my own or my family's detriment, they would not chastise me. Instead, they would nudge me toward caring for myself *as well as my family* while offering gentle advice about how I might support my loved ones more effectively. They wouldn't stand back and judge me; they would lean in to help.

In my world, people who take time out of their own lives to help an ailing or physically disabled loved one are called angels. They are amazing, wonderful, and special people. We need more of them.

Unfortunately, things are very different when it comes to addiction.

In contrast to the story above, let's say my spouse of twelve years became addicted to alcohol and prescription painkillers after having surgery. Let's say she lost her job because she was drunk and high at work. Let's say that because of her addiction, I can no longer trust her to adequately care for our kids. Let's say I'm concerned about her driving to school to pick up our kids because I don't know when she is sober or not. What happens in this set of circumstances when I take that second job, stop going to the gym, stop hanging out with friends, eliminate my recreational activities, gain weight, and am tired all the time? What will they say about the fact that I can't seem to stop obsessing about her drinking and using, all while paying the family bills and caring for our children alone? Will my friends and family, my employer, my clergy, and my therapist support this degree of caregiving and caretaking in this situation, while also empathizing with my frustration and exhaustion?

Most likely not.

In the addiction world, support and therapy for me as a spouse, parent, friend or child of an addict typically involves judgmental head-shaking, *tut-tuts*, and expressions of concern focused on *my* dysfunctional attempts to love, save, rescue, and heal the family.

*Move over empathy; make way for judgment.*

Codependency is a universe where caregiving is often viewed as enmeshed, enabling, and controlling, while choosing to stick by an addicted loved one is seen more as a reflection of the caregiver's troubled past—meaning unresolved early-life trauma and abandonment issues—than an indication of love and bonding.

This does not make sense and troubles me deeply. If I love someone with a physical illness or a disability and I help that person and the rest of my family, even to my detriment, I'm a saint. But if I love and care for an addict in the same way, I am called out as enmeshed, enabling, controlling, and codependent. Even worse, I am told that my attempts to resolve this crisis (my codependency), is making everything worse, not better. I may also be told that I need to "get out of my disease" or "I am enabling the problem, thereby hurting myself and the addict." Thus, the best way to effectively help is for me to pull back from all my unhealthy rescuing and work on myself.

## THE STIGMA OF ADDICTION

Perhaps the difference in how we view caring for a loved one with a cancer diagnosis versus caring for an addicted loved one stems from the fact that addiction remains deeply stigmatized in our culture, viewed as a moral failing or a sign of inherent weakness. Our image of an addict as an emancipated person lying in an alley with a needle in their arm and no future persists, even though only a very small percentage of addicts fit this stereotype.

Moreover, our twentieth-century perception of "addiction as a family disease" implies that everyone in an addict's family is pathologically unwell. Thus, entire families are stigmatized by addiction, most often those closest to the addict.

Despite everything we now know about addiction—what causes it, why some people are more susceptible than others, and how to treat it—addiction is viewed in nearly every culture (and in most families) as shameful, and silence is encouraged. Because of this, spouses, parents, and others who care for addicted loved ones tend to suffer in silence, providing care as best they can but with little or no useful guidance. There's too little information, there's too much shame, there's "what will the neighbors say?" etc. So, families desperately work to "look good" on the outside while they collapse internally. When the issues are finally brought to light, the advice that loved ones often receive is to intervene and then detach to distance themselves from the problem and refocus on themselves. And woe to those who choose otherwise, as they will surely be blamed, shamed, and pathologized.

When these loving individuals do make their way to therapeutic support, either on their own or in conjunction with the addict's treatment, do we honor and celebrate their devoted efforts at caregiving for someone they love and then offer them support? Hardly. Instead, we near instantly assume they are enmeshed, enabling, controlling, and thus contributing to the problem. Then we give those people a label—codependent—one that sounds a lot like a diagnosis. Once labeled, these wounded, scared people are asked (at the height of a profound interpersonal crisis) to look at themselves and "their part" in the problem. They are told that they are ill, just like the addict, and they need to work on themselves so they can fix whatever it is they've been doing wrong that is inadvertently driving the addiction forward.

## HOW IS THIS HELPFUL?

Why pin the stigma of addiction on the addict's family as well as the addict? Why pathologize hard-working, deeply loving, intensely loyal, profoundly afraid, nearly exhausted loved ones as codependent or worse? Is this the kindest and most effective way to invite them into the healing process? Does this represent the empathetic, non-judgmental embrace that such people clearly need and deserve? No. Clearly it does not.

No wonder it's increasingly difficult to keep loved ones and family members of addicts engaged in treatment. These are individuals who've spent months or even years trying to keep the family afloat, with little thanks for their efforts, and now we're talking to them (or maybe at them) in ways that cause them to feel blamed, shamed, and at fault. For years, I have listened to therapists and counselors talking about how difficult it is to work with the wives, husbands, children, and parents of addicts. I consistently hear statements such as:

- They don't want to own up to their part in the problem.
- They view the addict as the sole source of the problem, and that makes it hard to help the whole family.
- They don't see how their attempts to caretake are making things worse.
- They may be sober, but they're every bit as sick as the addicts they love.

- They just can't stop rescuing and obsessing over the problem which causes more trouble than it solves.
- They are acting out their own issues to everyone's detriment.
- If they don't detach from him and just let him suffer with his addiction, they will drive him right back to using.

Ouch!

## LET'S TRY THIS ANOTHER WAY

What if loved ones of addicts aren't difficult or resistant people at all? What if they are understandably troubled because they find themselves powerless to stop an addiction that is taking their loved one away from them? What if the real problem is that they neither understand, nor do they relate to, being labeled as codependent? What if our primary treatment model has diminished and marginalized them in ways that simultaneously confuse and leave them feeling unnecessarily blamed and shamed? Why prejudge loved ones of addicts as codependent and therefore drivers of a dysfunctional family system? What if that "diagnosis" pushes them into a reactionary state where they feel they must defend their actions to us while, in their minds, the actual problem lies with the addict themselves? And

> What if loved ones of addicts aren't difficult or resistant people at all? What if they are understandably troubled because they find themselves powerless to stop an addiction that is taking their loved one away from them? What if the real problem is that they neither understand, nor do they relate to, being labeled as codependent? What if our primary treatment model has diminished and marginalized them in ways that simultaneously confuse and leave them feeling unnecessarily blamed and shamed?

then we all end up going round and round, playing pin-the-tail on the pathology.

Why do addiction treatment professionals choose to initiate therapeutic relationships with painfully overwhelmed and under-supported loved ones of addicts by thrusting a negative, pathological sheen onto their more than generous caregiving?

Once they have formally been assigned a label, then they are expected to not only embrace this concept but to start working on it immediately. And when they act out against this model, therapists and others view them as difficult and unwilling to grow, which rein-forces the unsubstantiated belief that somehow they are as innately troubled as the addict. What about their grief for how their lives have turned out? What about their years of feeling confused, anxious, overwhelmed, and fearful about the future of an addict who they love? What about the fact that they have been victimized in their own homes, sometimes for years on end, by an addict who is more willing to lie, manipulate, and keep secrets than tell the truth?

Even when caregiving loved ones have been "doing it all wrong," experience tells us that it's not useful for anyone to blame them in any way for facilitating and perpetuating someone else's dysfunction. As a matter of fact, why would we say this at all? If you were exhausting yourself working part-time jobs in three different places while taking care of multiple people, including an active addict who is spending money faster than you can make it, would you feel engaged by a mes-sage that asks you to start looking at *your* problem? Most likely not. Instead, this concept would likely feel more hurtful and counterintui-tive than empathic.

If our sole approach toward helping loved ones of addicts alienates them before they can take advantage of the care and insight offered them, then maybe it's time to change our methodology. Forty years after the term codependency was coined, perhaps it's time to uncover more empathetic and compassionate ways to view such caregivers. Instead of blaming them for resisting a codependent path that feels innately wrong, perhaps it's time to explore less judgmental, less intrusive and more effective models that will help us to better understand and support them.

## MEETING PEOPLE WHERE THEY ARE

The process for therapists and others to build an empathetic connection with loved ones of addicts can be summed up by the oft-used social-work phrase "be where the client is." Therapists, counselors, and clergy are routinely taught to closely track what the person in front of them is saying/doing/expressing/feeling and then follow that person's intents, beliefs, and experiences. What we don't do is start with our assumptions. When we get this part right, everyone feels safer and better understood. The simple act of being empathetic and curious about another's experience, while simultaneously setting opinions and judgments aside, demonstrates in real time that we care about and want to understand in this person's world as they experience it.

## EMPATHY IN ACTION

No matter how distracted or out of touch we might get when supporting those we love, we can refocus on the work at hand by concentrating on what our struggling loved one is expressing. Simply put, we need to get out of our own heads and listen to what they need from us. In my experience, quick judgments are counterproductive to building a healing alliance. This means that those I am trying to support need to know me more as the guy who leaves them feeling understood, safe, usefully directed, motivated, and hopeful rather than as the guy who points out what's wrong with them and pushes them toward change. To support those we love, we need to be curious and empathetic rather than offering quick solutions based on our own feelings and beliefs. *Not every person who is struggling wants or needs to gain insight or change their behaviors; sometimes they just want to be heard.*

This vitally important therapy-sourced concept simply means that none of us (professional or not) should verbalize assumptions or ideas about how to help someone before that person has fully shown, from their perspective, exactly what they need. Until then, unless there is an emergency, we keep our ideas, suggestions, directions, beliefs, and assumptions to ourselves as we go about understanding and relating. So, again, and I cannot state this any more clearly, the foundation of our attempts to help anyone is an empathetic, nonjudgmental relationship where that person feels both understood and supported.

Do I always agree with everything someone tells me? No, I don't, especially when I am working with addicts themselves. Depending on the circumstances, I may, when the time is right, disclose what I think. If the timing is not right, I keep my thoughts to myself. As a therapist, clergy, or friend my evaluations and goals must be rooted in concern, compassion, and empathy otherwise I'm unable to offer fully useful support. Without a respectful alliance, even our best intents and the most targeted advice is likely to fail.

# ADDICTS IN TREATMENT

Those seeking addiction treatment and related help from loved ones need to be seen, heard, and responded to based on what they say, think, and feel. That said, the information that an active addict tells us is not nearly as important as the awareness gained by observing their actions. When seeking useful insight into an addict's world, their behaviors tell us far more than their words.

Simply stated, active addicts are steeped in denial. They will insist, despite their addictive behavior patterns and the many consequences with which they are currently dealing, that they are doing just fine. They say that they deeply love their spouse, kids, job, home, church, friends, etc., and would never do anything to jeopardize that. Yet when offered a chance to get high or act out a behavioral addiction, they will nearly always choose that path over protecting the people, places, and things they profess to love and care about. Still, it's all under control as far as they are concerned.

What addicts tell a therapist and nearly everyone else in their lives about what they feel, want and need most often does not align with their life choices and behaviors. A good friend, loved one or professional must recognize and see this in order to be truly helpful. And as every informed twelve-step sponsor or counselor will say: *that's how we meet addicted clients where they are.*

Untreated addicts are out of control. By the time they get to therapy or treatment, their obsession with their drug or behavior of choice has pushed the arc of their lives (and the lives of everyone close to them) askew. They are wobbling, out of balance, or worse. Therefore, guiding them toward healing means encouraging them to see and accept the truth of their situation while providing structure, education, support, and accountability.

## LOVED ONES IN TREATMENT

As stated above, helping an active addict get and stay clean involves breaking through their denial while introducing containment, structure, guidance, support, and accountability (whether the addict wants it or not). But what about the needs of those who love an addict? Do such people also need containment, structure, and accountability, or do their emotional needs differ? What do these fearful, hurting, betrayed individuals need from others who care about them? Prodependence says they need support, direction, and hope from day one rather than being pushed toward self-examination or self-criticism.

## TRAUMA BONDS

Prodependence does not agree with the concept that anyone bonds or stays with an addict primarily as a form of trauma repetition. Rather, the model suggests that we choose to remain with such people because we love them and see within these relationships an opportunity for all to grow and mature. No more, no less. Prodependence does not suggest that we are required to examine our own motivations and history in order to help an addict get sober. Could all of us benefit by taking the road of self-examination and insight? Of course. But this is useful only if we choose to grow and become more self-aware for ourselves or to improve our relationships—not to fix someone else. This is the primary message of prodependence: that we remain and help troubled others primarily out of love and by doing so we will all heal faster and more effectively together than we can alone. Prodependence doesn't view loved ones of addicts as inevitable victims of their own traumatic past now repeating itself in their adult lives. But rather they are viewed under this model as valiant individuals struggling to love another person even in the face of addiction.

To be clear, the concept of prodependence agrees with the fact that all us humans will recreate the emotional dynamics of our childhoods in adult lives at some point or another. And this makes sense because those dynamics are what we know and that are most familiar to us from our earliest days. Nearly all current psychological research and treatment methods related to early-life trauma tells us that this is true. The people we choose as adult partners along with some of the ways we rear our own children or love our own parents will always be somewhat reflective of our own past. How could it not? But does that translate into the codependent belief that we are destined to choose and stay with an addict because of our own pathology? No. That concept is the antithesis of what prodependence is all about. Are we attracted to people at a similar level of emotional functioning as ourselves? Sure. Will most of us do nearly anything to ensure the safety and sanity of our children, parents or other people we love? You bet. Do we get involved or stay with them because we are unconsciously setting ourselves up for failure and deception as we may have experienced in the past? No way. We get involved or stay because of the connection we share with them. The new model discussed through the remainder of this book called *Prodependence* suggests that we remain connected to such people not only out of love, but also because we sense that remaining together, in both good times and bad, offers all of us an opportunity to thrive.

# Chapter Two

# INTRODUCING PRODEPENDENCE

*Progress is impossible without change,*
*and those who cannot change their minds*
*cannot change anything.*

—George Bernard Shaw

**P**rodependence is a term created to describe attachment relationships that are healthfully interdependent, where one person's strengths support the vulnerabilities of the other and vice versa, with this mutual support occurring automatically and without question. This concept is specifically intended to focus on addicts and their families as that remains one of the few therapeutic and personally supportive arenas where codependency continues to be actively promoted.

Prodependence turns codependence 180 degrees, choosing to celebrate and take healthful advantage of a caregiving loved one's need and willingness to support and stay connected with an addict. Prodependence implies no shame or blame, no sense of being wrong, no language that pathologizes such caregiving loved ones. Instead, there is recognition for effort given, plus hope and useful instruction for healing.

## WHY PRODEPENDENCE?

Prodependence (unlike codependence) views the emotional reactivity and impulsive behaviors of an active addict's loved ones as an understandable, normative response, one that anyone might have when helplessly watching someone they love fall apart. Prodependence (unlike codependence) doesn't view them as inherently broken but more as people who are being broken down by their inability to fix a deeply troubled addict. In therapy talk, we say that such people are facing a situational crisis. And let's face it, anyone who feels helpless to stop the additive nightmare that is rolling out right in front of them can look kinda crazy. That makes sense. But again, the concept does not imply that those who chose to love or remain with an addict do so because their own challenging past has inevitably led them to seek out or embrace a crisis-driven life.

As stated, we can view the actions and words of those who are emotionally connected to an addict—helpful or unhelpful— as a healthy response to an interpersonal crisis. Prodependence does not agree that anyone's words or actions can ever lead another person to abuse substances or behaviors. Let's say that again. No one can make someone else abuse drugs, drink or act out—period! People do not act out addictively because someone else's issues or behaviors are "driving their addiction" and/or "driving them crazy." Addicts universally act out because that's what they want to do. They may and will blame others for their addiction, but those beliefs are driven more out of their desire to make anyone else be the cause of "the problem" rather than themselves. Externalizing your addiction by blaming it on someone else is useful for those who are unable or unwilling to look at themselves as the root of their own problems. After all, if you are able to view others as the source of your misery, then you never have to take responsibility for it!

Unlike the existing, dominant codependency model, prodependence views the relationship between an addict and someone they love, despite the presence of addiction, as being healthfully interdependent, where one person's strengths fill in the vulnerabilities of the other and vice versa. Further, prodependence suggests that this mutual support is no more and no less than an expression of meaningful love and attachment, a relational pattern that occurs near automatically and is not to be pathologized. As applied to caregivers of addicts, prodependence refers to the extraordinarily loving attempts taken by a loved one to heal an addict to whom they are deeply attached and bonded.

Rather than blaming, shaming, and pathologizing the family and friends of addicts for "loving too much" or not in the right way, or for self-focused reasons, prodependence celebrates their need to love and to caretake when appropriate.

The rationale underlying prodependence pushes back against viewing a loved one's struggles as a form of pathology (sourced in early-life trauma reactivity), but rather as a normative response anyone might demonstrate when in the midst of an interpersonal crisis. The primary hypothesis underlying prodependence holds that of course they are acting this way because they are emotionally exhausted and overwhelmed. We suggest that when facing such situations and losses, who among us would not act a little crazy? Why would we judge people who are in the middle of a relationship crisis?

Unlike codependence, prodependence does not view them as reacting to past trauma but rather as people understandably responding to their painful current circumstances. Codependency insists that the reason loved ones act out is due to their own early hurts, pain, and traumatic losses being repeated. Prodependence says that anyone would act and feel a little nutty when in crisis—no more and no less.

Prodependence views the act of loving and trying to help an addict or a similarly troubled individual heal (or just to make it through the day without creating yet another mess) as an indicator of healthy attachment and loving connection. Prodependent treatment offers loved ones recognition for their support in addition to hope and useful instruction for healing. To treat loved ones of addicts using prodependence, we need not find that something is "wrong with them." We can simply acknowledge the trauma and inherent dysfunction that occurs when living in close relationship with an addict, and then we can address that in the healthiest, least shaming way.

> To treat loved ones of addicts using prodependence, we need not find that something is "wrong with them." We can simply acknowledge the trauma and inherent dysfunction that occurs when living in close relationship with an addict, and then we can address that in the healthiest, least shaming way.

As with codependence, prodependence recognizes that when a caregiver's actions run off the rails and become counterproductive, measures can be taken to put the relationship healing back on track.

However, prodependence does not imply that a caregiver's dysfunctional behaviors arise out of any of their own past or present trauma or pathology. Instead, prodependence views their actions as understandable attempts to maintain or restore healthy attachment. Prodependence does not ever consider efforts made to help a loved one get well as a form of illness, even if those attempts to help are misdirected and ineffective. Under no circumstances does prodependence imply that love is or can become pathological. This is not a model that would ever tell someone that they can "love too much." Instead, prodependence acknowledges that loving an unpredictable, addicted partner who blames, lies, seduces, manipulates, and gaslights can make pretty much anyone look and act kinda crazy over time. To this point, just because people in crisis look and sometimes act like they have lost their minds, it doesn't mean that they have. Prodependence pushes back against the concept that caregivers are acting out their own issues thereby making the problem worse.

## PRODEPENDENT CARE IS FOCUSED ON HERE AND NOW

Interestingly, prodependence recommends and implements similar outcomes as does codependence: a fresh or renewed focus on self-care coupled with implementation of healthier boundaries. That said, the two models approach this work from vastly different perspectives. Codependence, as a deficit-based trauma model, views loved ones of addicts as acting out of their own damaged past for which they need help from day one. Prodependence, as a strength-based, attachment-driven model, views loved ones of addicts as people in the midst of a life crisis (addiction in a loved one), one that they have little training or ability to resolve on their own.

Prodependence does not ask these people to engage in therapy or recovery for deep inner reflection or to examine their current problems in relationship to past trauma. From the start, the model asks us to not question, blame, judge, or diagnose such loved ones based on their efforts to help. If you think about it, we don't know who that person was or how they acted before active addiction showed up in their lives. This is why counseling professionals are taught that it is unethical to diagnose anyone who is experiencing an acute crisis.

Prodependence says that meeting this client where they are means that the therapy method chosen to help them must mirror their current problems and not their past—no more and no less. In such situations, what is the purpose of exploring past traumas from the start? There is plenty of trauma to go around here and now if you love an active addict. When working with them, as any client, therapists are encouraged to start their work with them by looking for any chronic physical or mental health problems (depression, anxiety, addictions, OCD, etc.) at the start. After that, the therapist's job is to simply sit with these people, learn what they need, and actively help them—all in the here and now. Thus, from the get-go, prodependent therapy tells them some form of the following:

"You are such a strong and loving person for putting all this time and effort into helping your addicted loved one. Despite all of your intensely focused attempts to get them sober, your hard work has not yet resulted in them becoming sober. But who could ever blame you for trying your best, after all these are not typical circumstances. After all, it's not that you studied addiction treatment 101 in high school." Watching your spouse or child get sicker by the day while being impotent to help them is a nightmare for any of us. Let's face it, there is no way to do your loving and intimate best in the middle of a disaster zone. If the house is burning down, you grab your loved one and drag that person out of the fire, and you don't worry about whether you're grabbing too hard or in a way that hurts.

Prodependent treatment with caregiving loved ones of addicts recognizes and accepts, first and foremost, that these individuals are in crisis and are likely to behave accordingly. As such, they will show emotional lability and overwhelm. They may also exert superhuman effort to manage household chores, childcare, doctors' visits, home healthcare, and earn extra money to make up for the active addict's deficits. Most importantly, we need to validate the fact that they have behaved in these ways in a vain attempt to maintain stability and not to recreate early pathology. They may be in grief, they may express remorse, fear or rage—and understandably so, therefore the ways they express such feelings should never be pathologized, but rather be validated and normalized.

The prodependence model encourages therapists, clergy, twelve-step participants, family, and friends to help these people by celebrating what we all share—a natural and healthy need to maintain our intimate connections and to protect our loved ones. We should celebrate (not judge) their desire and attempts to provide ongoing, uninterrupted support even to their own deficit when facing down addiction or similar interpersonal crisis.

## WORDS MATTER

In many respects, the prodependence and codependence models have similar end goals but with a profound difference. The ways they vary from one another is defined by how we frame the problem.

Consider the following graph delineating traits that are often seen in loved ones of addicts. In the left-hand column are the negative-sounding words that most often get thrown about when we discuss codependence. The right-hand column lists similar traits but reframed as prodependent positives.

## Language of Codependence Versus Prodependence

| CODEPENDENT LANGUAGE | PRODEPENDENT LANGUAGE |
|---|---|
| Enmeshed | Deeply involved |
| Externally focused | Concerned about the welfare of others |
| Enabling | Supportive and engaged |
| Fearful | Deeply concerned about the health, stability and future of those they love |
| Lacking healthy boundaries | Eager to care for a loved one |
| Can't say no | Says yes to every opportunity to help |
| Obsessed with the addiction | Determined to protect the addict and their family |
| Living in denial | Unwilling to give up on someone they love |
| Angry | Frustrated that they can't convince their loved one to get help |
| Controlling | Trying to anticipate and manage serious problems before they reoccur |
| Hypervigilant | Watching for signs that the problem will reoccur or worsen |

To my thinking, one model imposes a pseudo-pathology that leaves many people feeling more broken than lifted up, while the other is positive and supportive with its focus on validating loving caregivers in the same ways that they see themselves.

Do loved ones of addicts always make the best decisions and go about the business of helping in the best possible way? Of course not. Do they occasionally overstep their bounds in ways that are harmful? Of course they do. But why would we expect anything different from a person who is trying with all their might to effect change in a situation where none is forthcoming. The simple truth is that loved ones of active addicts are perpetually in crisis mode. Naturally, they try to control the crisis. In the process, they sometimes panic and make bad decisions. They may overdo. They may help too much. They may help ineffectively. They may enable and appear to be pathologically enmeshed. They may regress to earlier states of functioning (past trauma.) But that does not mean they are suffering from their own psychological disorders. What it means is they are people in distress, behaving in the ways that people in distress tend to behave. Thus, anyone who is tasked to help these individuals must validate their experience and value their contributions while guiding them toward useful and effective solutions. We don't judge (or diagnose) anyone when they are in the middle of an unresolved crisis. In the therapy world,

> The simple truth is that loved ones of active addicts are perpetually in crisis mode. Naturally, they try to control the crisis. In the process, they sometimes panic and make bad decisions. They may overdo. They may help too much. They may help ineffectively. They may enable and appear to be pathologically enmeshed. They may regress to earlier states of functioning (past trauma.) But that does not mean they are suffering from their own psychological disorders.

doing that is considered unethical as the counselor does not know anything about who they were before these issues became acute. To do so is like asking someone why they are acting like a crazy person simply because their first born was just hit by a truck. No one would say there was something wrong with that parent for being a terrified mess. Why view loved ones of active addicts any differently?

## WHAT ABOUT THE PAST?

Once the crisis stage of active addiction is in the past, if someone wants to do deeper forms of inner work (like addressing unresolved trauma) that is a task some may choose to take on or not. That is up to them and them only. To be clear, in the world of addiction the crisis has passed if/when the addict gets sober and/or when they are out of your life. Once the dust of active addiction has passed, it's not unusual for some to say, "I'm beginning to wonder if anything about the way I grew up might relate to why I chose this person and/or how I was able to tolerate their dysfunction?"

However, encouraging someone to take on such deeper psychological work too soon can quickly lead an understandably overwhelmed person toward increased anxiety, self-doubt, and a gnawing sense that they are a contributor to the problem. In other words, it is counterproductive to helping this person return to healthy coping.

## WHY PRODEPENDENCE?

Family members and loved ones struggle with the fact that someone they care about is addicted. They also struggle with having to take on extra responsibilities of helping while forgoing personal pleasures and development. In an attempt to help, the people around them will frequently tell them:

- You have an unhealthy obsession with the addict.
- You are enmeshed with the addict.
- You are enabling the addiction.
- You don't express love in a healthy way.
- You are too close to the problem (addict).
- You are dysfunctionally trying to control the addict's thinking and behavior.
- You are making the problem worse.
- You are addicted to the addict themselves.

Advising such people to "stop rescuing" and to "detach with love" does not account for or even recognize the fact that they can't stop loving the people they love any more than they can stop breathing. Providing them with useful forms of advice and direction means teaching them how to give of themselves in ways that are more productive and less stressful for all concerned. Rather than telling these folks they are an intrinsic part of the problem, we can lead them toward improved self-care and more effective caregiving while offering them our loving direction and assistance. Telling someone in such circumstances that they are enmeshed and enabling and need to detach can be a disaster for all concerned. Consider the following true story:

> Evan, a forty-eight-year-old single father, learned that his seventeen-year-old son, Oliver, was actively abusing heroin and had been since he was fifteen. From the moment Evan found out about his son's drug use, he blamed himself (and his failed marriage) and, out of love for his son

and guilt for their past, he did everything he could think of to help. He sent the young man to rehabs, tolerated his stealing from their home to buy drugs, paid his rent after he moved out of the house, and paid for college even though Oliver spent more time getting high than going to class.

When Oliver was twenty, Evan took a good look at how his efforts were paying off, saw no progress, and finally took his therapist's, his CoDA sponsor's, his friends' and family members' advice to disengage from Oliver to let him struggle on his own, that he would never fully take responsibility for his own life while his father was continuously rescuing him. Evan strongly disagreed with this advice as it didn't feel right to him as a father. But acknowledging that his efforts to date had clearly failed, he surrendered to the idea of letting go and leaving his son to struggle on his own.

Within a year, Oliver was homeless, arrested for theft, and sent to prison for eighteen months. Throughout this ordeal, Evan was continually coached to detach with love and to only give to Oliver when he is sober and doing the right thing. Still, Evan couldn't help but worry about Oliver's safety and wellbeing, concerns that dominated his days and left him sleepless at night.

When Oliver was released from prison, Evan wanted to get him into a drug rehab instead of the depressing halfway house to which he'd been assigned, but again he was advised to remain disengaged to let Evan struggle on his own. And that is exactly what he did. Unfortunately, Oliver was unable to find a decent job, became depressed, started using again, and ended up back on the streets. A week before his twenty-third birthday he overdosed and died just a few miles from his father's home.

When I first heard about this story from a colleague, I couldn't help but wonder what might have happened had Evan been coached using prodependence as his guide. Had he been directed toward maintaining a supportive, well-boundaried relationship with his son—no matter what—perhaps Oliver would have had someone around to catch him before his final fall. Perhaps there would have been a system in place to look out for him—sober or not.

It's easy to counsel a parent in a situation like this toward separation from this painful problem, leading with well-worn tropes such as, "Your son is a man now, and his decisions are his own," or, "You have given him all you can, but now you need to let him sink or swim on his own," or, "We all have to let go sometime." While this may feel like sensible advice to those offering it, when an addict goes to prison or dies because we have encouraged detachment rather than well-defined, ongoing connection, loved ones may spend a lifetime wondering if they could have done more. Some will forever blame themselves for the addict's tragic consequences.

> While this may feel like sensible advice to those offering it, when an addict goes to prison or dies because we have encouraged detachment rather than well-defined, ongoing connection, loved ones may spend a lifetime wondering if they could have done more. Some will forever blame themselves for the addict's tragic consequences.

Consider this question: Who gets to decide when it's time to give up on someone you love? Or this one: Who wants to be the therapist, friend, or clergy who advised Evan to let his son go only to have that direction lead to Oliver's untimely death?

With prodependence as a guide, it's entirely possible that Evan would have gotten Oliver into a rehab after prison, and in time Oliver would have found sobriety, a job, and grown into a relatively healthy and well-adjusted person. We have all seen such healing occur even under the most unlikely and unexpected of circumstances. You just never know when or how someone will finally be able to shift the focus of their lives from dysfunction to health.

Why label or pathologize primary supporters of challenged individuals who refuse to abandon or diminish their care giving for someone they love? What we can do is provide them with an outline for engaging in self-care while developing and maintaining healthy boundaries. We can usefully offer a structure that allows them to continue to love unconditionally without undue enabling, controlling, or doing things the addicted one could and should do for themselves.

Prodependence asks us to revisit pre-existing ideas related to codependency like caregiving, and caretaking with the introduction of a fresh, non-shaming, attachment-based paradigm for mutually effective and healthy support.

Prodependence chooses to celebrate a caregiver's desire to love and support an addicted family member—period.

## WHY PRODEPENDENCE MATTERS

Addicts cope with stress, depression, anxiety, loneliness, boredom, excitement, and unresolved trauma by getting high or acting out. They choose addictive substances and behaviors over people. They fear emotional intimacy and refuse to turn to others—even loved ones—when they're struggling. Instead, they self-soothe and escape by numbing out with addictive substances or behaviors.

Over time, to displace such destructive coping mechanisms, addicts must develop healthy ego strength and self-esteem via strong social support—prodependent connections with fellow recovering addicts and loving, empathic others. Ongoing connection to healthful others, especially those closest to them is the most effective weapon in the sobriety toolbox. When we teach an addict how and when to engage, utilize, and maintain healthy interpersonal support, we give them the keys to staying sober over time.

# Chapter Three

# THE ORIGINS OF CODEPENDENCY

*I want to grow. I want to be better.*
*You grow. We all grow. We're made to grow.*
*You either evolve or you disappear.*

—Tupac Shakur[1]

I f we are to view the "diagnosis" of codependency as a pop-culture phenomenon rather than a psychological truth, then we must fully understand the origins of the model itself. After all, codependence wasn't created in a vacuum. Its creation and popularity was both a reflection of the times and a reaction to the personal experiences of those who created it.

# WHY CODEPENDENCE BECAME POPULAR

From a therapy perspective, four significant mid-twentieth century psychotherapeutic and cultural shifts preceded and then fed the inception and development of codependence:

1) Humanistic psychotherapy
2) Recognition of early-life trauma
3) The women's movement
4) Addiction as a family disease (systems theory)

## Humanistic Psychotherapy

From the early 1960s onward, humanistic psychotherapy pushed the counseling field to focus clients on the idea of self-actualization, which is, essentially, the process of realizing one's full potential in life. Humanistic psychotherapy encourages us to focus on personal achievement and growth as our primary source of strength. It encourages self-awareness and mindfulness as a way of changing one's thinking and behaviors. Part revelation, part revolution, humanistic psychology is focused more on ego-strength, self-awareness, and interpersonal relating than illness. This new work then offered therapists and their clients a more holistic view of human potential and was, without a doubt, a freeing experience for both therapists and clients. Throughout the 1970s and 1980s, this new approach trickled down into popular culture via countless thousands of seekers—people then flocking to self-help programs and self-improvement seminars such as EST (Erhard Seminars Training), Lifespring, Insight, and Landmark, each presenting a propriety mix of activities and exercises designed to help individuals *self-actualize*. These various attempts at self-actualization mirrored other popular movements of the era. These included Eastern philosophies, twelve-step recovery, group therapy, and the exploration of psychedelics and other drugs as a means toward evolving consciousness. Goodbye ties, jackets, and Frank Sinatra; hello tie-dye, long hair, and rock and roll. Self-expression, rather than following cultural "norms," became a predominant theme of the times. *Ahh,* the 1960s.

The defining concepts of humanistic psychology are perhaps best summarized by psychologist Tom Greening, who states:

- Human beings, as human, supersede the sum of their parts. They cannot be reduced to components.
- Human beings have their existence in a uniquely human context, as well as in a cosmic ecology.
- Human beings are aware and are aware of being aware—i.e. they are conscious. Human consciousness always includes an awareness of oneself in the context of other people.
- Human beings have the ability to make choices and therefore have responsibility.
- Human beings are intentional, aim at goals, are aware that they cause future events, and seek meaning, value, and creativity.[2]

Pretty trippy, huh? Needless to say, this perspective was a sea change from the stuffy, relatively non-relational "therapist as a blank slate" psychoanalytic and behaviorist movements that preceded it. This focus on human potential rather than human pathology also opened the door to viewing addicts as troubled people with an innate and intact capacity to grow and heal rather than hopelessly broken people.

## Recognition of Early-Life Trauma

As the humanistic psychology movement was gaining steam, researchers of the era also began looking at the effects of early- and later-life emotional trauma on adult life. Prior to this era, traumatized individuals wanting to understand their feelings were most often diagnosed as weak-willed and inherently emotionally unhealthy. Only rarely did therapy professionals consider the impact of their potentially overwhelming life experiences. Sadly, therapists of the era had little to no insight, training, or understanding of the wide-ranging, long-lasting effects caused by trauma. They mostly avoided the issue or viewed it as a sign of lifelong mental illness.

The trauma field took a big leap forward in the late 1960s as war-hardened Vietnam veterans returned home, manifesting multiple profound emotional, psychological, and behavioral problems—including addiction. The impact of the war on these men was significant and undeniable. They went to Vietnam healthy and whole; they returned from the war beaten and broken. And it wasn't just the soldiers who identified this change; their friends and families also noticed a huge difference. The evolving research of that time then lead to the creation of a formal trauma-sourced diagnosis that we now call PTSD (post-traumatic stress disorder).

This groundbreaking diagnosis identified four primary symptoms:

1) Re-experiencing trauma—in flashbacks, nightmares, and even in response to loud noises and stressful situations.

2) Numbed or dissociative response as a way of coping with the pain of the past.

3) Hypervigilance—anxiety, psychological arousal, jumpiness, overreactions, etc.

4) Anhedonia—a profound and persistent inability to experience joy.

Recognizing this new clinical reality, scholars such as Christine Courtois, Bessel van der Kolk, and John Briere then began to ask,

"Can the symptoms we see with combat veterans also manifest in the general population in response to other forms of non-combat related PTSD?" Their answer was an undeniable yes. The new diagnosis of PTSD evoked new questions. Might those same types of symptoms manifest in those whose lives have been deeply affected by trauma that is unrelated to war? Could symptoms like those above also result from the trauma of sexual abuse, domestic violence, racial intolerance, homophobia, gender discrimination, cultural violations, violent crime, misogyny, bullying, neglect and chronic family dysfunction?

In her writings, Dr. Courtois defines trauma as "any event or experience (including witnessing) that is physically and/or psychologically overwhelming to the exposed individual."[3] She also states that trauma has both objective and subjective dimensions, meaning trauma "can involve just about any type of profound adversity or harm, and a person's response is dependent on their individualized experience, perspective, and temperament."[4] In other words, people can react very differently to the same situation. For instance, a new mother with her infant child in the car would likely be more profoundly traumatized by a fender bender than a professional race car driver.

My point here is simple. Starting in the late 1960s, we began to explore and understand the now well-accepted idea that trauma, no matter how it occurs, can have both immediate and long-lasting effects, such as:

- Flashbacks
- Nightmares
- Anxiety
- Depression
- Hypervigilance

- Stress
- Shame
- Lowered self-esteem
- Challenges in developing and maintaining meaningful emotional intimacy
- Physical illness
- Rage/violence
- Addictions

Today, we readily acknowledge the link between early-life trauma and numerous later-life symptoms and disorders. An immense amount of research has confirmed this link. One study looking at the long-term effects of those people with unresolved early-life trauma versus those without. They found that in relation to people who have not experienced trauma, trauma survivors are:

- 1.8 times more likely to smoke cigarettes
- 1.9 times more likely to become obese
- 2.4 times more likely to experience ongoing anxiety
- 3.6 times more likely to be depressed
- 3.6 times more likely to qualify as promiscuous
- 7.2 times more likely to become alcoholic
- 11.1 times more likely to become an intravenous drug user[5]

A defining belief reinforced repeatedly in "codependency work" is a primary focus on the exploration of early-life trauma. The theory unquestionably states that people who deeply bond and remain with an active addict must themselves be acting "crazy" because they are re-enacting aspects of their own traumatic past. And further, if/when their deeply traumatizing past has been explored and worked though that it will no longer be an engine for their *codependent reactivity.* In the therapy field we define this concept as trauma repetition.

## The Women's Movement

Up until the very recent past, flawed clinical research and related therapies for women closely mirrored the negative religious and related societal norms of their time. In one brief example, consider the Victorian era, when nearly any woman who was openly expressing strong emotions and opinions was seen to be hysterical. At that time, women were supposed to be subtle, non-intrusive, and demure, i.e., "the gentler sex" and never shrill, intrusive, or outspoken. Given this culturally bound framework, women who did not fit the mold were told that there was something wrong with them.

By the early 1960s, women all around the United States and the world were increasingly frustrated with and vocal about the cultural and legal limitations placed on their social and economic status. As women were striving to have their voices heard in a man's world, they were strongly encouraged to embrace traditionally male character traits of individualism, aggression and being highly competitive. The goal was unquestionably to beat men at their own game.

Throughout the 1960s and 1970s, women carried the message of those times into the workplace and beyond, by doubling down in their efforts to be more assertive and competitive in order to gain equality with men. Think about the wonderfully entertaining 1980 movie *9 to 5.* In this film, three female employees working for a sexist, lying, hypocritical male bigot turn the tables and take control of their workplace (committing about a hundred very funny felonies in the process). At the time, much of this film's appeal centered around its timely feminist theme. In fact, this early "girl power" film nicely represents the progressive steps forward that women were trying to take and the ways in which they were going about it—in this case, by one-upping their male boss and beating him at his own game.

The fact that so many women identified with the plot of *9 to 5* indicates how profoundly disempowered women of the era felt. And the film also very clearly illustrates that they determined the best way to get ahead likely sounded something like this: "If you want to succeed in a man's world, act more like a man!" If getting ahead meant being more assertive, more individualistic, more direct, and less empathic toward others, so be it. Thus, at the time, women were strongly encouraged to consciously and deliberately be less dependent on anyone for their own validation income, survival, happiness, and the like.

The codependence movement, once introduced, took off like a rocket because, in concert with the women's rights movements that preceded it, codependence encouraged women to focus on their own self-development by eliminating their tendency to lean into *unhealthy, caregiving dependencies*. This translated into the addiction world by telling women that by giving deeply of themselves to focus on a broken, needful loved one (read man), they were holding themselves back from becoming their best selves. Women of the era were told that personal growth required detaching and distancing from the addicts in their lives by letting the addicted person alone to figure it out on their own.

This new approach to relating gave women permission to differentiate as individuals by taking control of their own lives while simultaneously releasing control over their addicted loved ones. And this message spoke volumes to women seeking equality in the 1980s, with its message of personal empowerment through detachment. Many a glass ceiling was shattered by women who embraced these ideas. And more power to them. Unfortunately, these concepts also reinforce an antidependent message that encourages going it alone, rather than leaning into others, for shared support and affiliation.

Melody Beattie from *Codependent No More*:

> Detach. Detach in love, detach in anger, but strive for detachment. I know it's difficult, but it will become easier with practice. If you can't let go completely, try to "hang on loose." Relax. Sit back. Now, take a deep breath. The focus is on you.[6]

Many decades later, this advice, though in a somewhat altered and more strident form, remains the primary message carried by those still invested in the codependency movement.

---

## Dysfunction Gets Trendy

By the early 1980s, the once deeply personal and private stories of addiction and emotional trauma (the long-hidden realities of mental illness, addiction, and profound family dysfunction) burst on the public scene in a big way. Once out of the closet, such issues almost immediately became powerful fodder for pop-culture entertainment, delivered to the masses in the form of daytime television talk shows. Starting then and still going strong today, the painful face of real human tragedy has provided trendy viewing candy. Why watch the manufactured pain of actors in soap opera scripts—the other popular form of daytime televised entertainment—when you could suddenly watch real people's real pain play out in real time? These formerly private discussions, suddenly made public, turned many a TV personality into a name brand—Phil Donahue, Sally Jessy Raphael, Dr. Phil, Dr. Drew, Oprah, and many others. As wacky as some of these shows might have seemed, they nonetheless offered many people the comfort of not being alone in their problems while also preaching the codependent gospel as a solution to most relational problems.

As the trauma movement grew, therapists began to see the relationship between abusive and neglectful early-life experiences and later-life addictions and mental illness. This clinical insight into trauma and its effect on human functionality has allowed us entry into the pain and confusion suffered by so many seeking relief. This is the basic idea of trauma. It happens to us, and it happens to those we love. And if we don't find a way to recognize it, call it out, and get support for working through it, such issues will color our thinking and behavior indefinitely.

## Addiction as a Family Disease (Systems Theory)

The twentieth century's implementation of the disease model of addiction was, in many respects, a wonderful thing. Addicts were no longer vilified as personality disordered bums and losers, providing counselors with a useful, non-moralistic medical model to implement in treatment.

Unfortunately, systems theory, a set of beliefs that views the family as a conglomeration of interrelated parts, over time became conflated with the disease model of addiction. By applying systems theory to the disease of addiction, our thinking shifted from seeing that individual (the addict) as the source of their own problems, to viewing the addict's family and close social relationships as being a primary contributor to the problem and not part of the solution. Suddenly, everyone in the family was seen as playing a meaningful and troubling role in the formation and maintenance of addiction. We went from focusing on the disease of the addiction itself to focusing on the disease of the entire family.

But what is this "family disease"? With addicts, the primary manifestation of the disease of addiction was obviously their obsession with their drug or behavior of choice. With family members, things weren't so clear.

> By applying systems theory to the disease of addiction, our thinking shifted from seeing that individual (the addict) as the source of their own problems, to viewing the addict's family and close social relationships as being a primary contributor to the problem and not part of the solution. Suddenly, everyone in the family was seen as playing a meaningful and troubling role in the formation and maintenance of addiction.

The general thinking seemed to be that if the addict's disease centered on obsession, so did the family's, so therapists decided to view the family's disease as an obsession, not with the addictive substance, but with the addicts themselves.

As the 1980s progressed, partners and other loved ones of addicts were increasingly viewed as contributing to the formation and maintenance of addiction. And the family's enabling, fixing, controlling, and unhelpful behaviors seen as detrimental; an unhealthy obsession with the addict and their behavior (see John Bradshaw's work, *Bradshaw On: The Family*).

Scholarly concepts about the etiology between family/loved ones and the addiction itself came to a crossroads. Below are the two versions of these same issues:

1) The impact of addiction on loved ones and family members viewed them as adaptive survivors of an addictive process.

2) The impact of loved ones and family members on the addiction, viewing them as active contributors to addictive process.

The first path (prodependence) acknowledges that loved ones of addicts are traumatized individuals reacting to a painful crisis. This also recognizes that the addict's highly dysfunctional, sometimes abusive, addiction-driven behaviors *are the primary source* of the family's immediate pain and trauma. The second path seems to be where our thinking went awry (codependence). Here, the onus of addiction was seen as resulting from the actions of "enmeshed, troubled, and controlling" family members in addition to an addict's underlying trauma.[7]

Unfortunately, the second path is the one the addiction field seemed to grab onto. Because of this, as the disease model of addiction came into vogue, so did the "codependent" blaming and shaming of family members, especially wives. Wives of addicts pre-codependency were routinely viewed, judged, and labeled as psychologically unhealthy women who chose men predisposed toward addiction. Sadly, there is nothing new about our applying a negative label to committed female caregivers. To this point, prominent addiction historian William White is quoted below referring to the common assumptions made about the wives of alcoholics in the 1930s through the 1950s.

> The general profile of the alcoholic wife depicted in this early literature was that of a woman who was neurotic, sexually repressed, dependent, man-hating, domineering, mothering, guilty and masochistic, and/ or hostile and nagging. The typical therapist's view of the wife of the alcoholic was generally one of "I'd drink, too, if I were married to her."[8]

When viewed from this perspective, the very concept of codependency can be seen as another, if more evolved, way of shaming and devaluing angry, loving, and frightened spouses and loved ones. Sadly, this model considers their fully understandable reactions and behaviors related to an addicted loved one as examples of their own pathology or illness.

In opposition to such beliefs, prodependence would say these concepts are nothing more than a sophisticated way to blame those victimized by addiction.

When working with loved ones of addicts, I encourage a shift in thinking from codependence to prodependence. Loved ones of addicts need to see themselves as the compassionate and committed people they are. We need to acknowledge that these are loving, whole people doing their best to support a troubled person whom they love. They're not inherently broken people. What they are is intact, loving human beings who are in the midst of a relationship crisis. By moving beyond the negative judgments brought about by the codependency model, we can view these well-intentioned people through a lens of love and strength as opposed to trauma repetition and gender-biased expectations.

## Chapter Four

# THE PROBLEM WITH CODEPENDENCY

*It is a capital mistake to theorize before one has data.*
*Insensibly one begins to twist facts to suit theories,*
*instead of theories to suit facts.*

—Sir Arthur Conan Doyle, *Sherlock Holmes*

**Codependence:** A psychological condition or a relationship in which a person is controlled or manipulated by another who is affected with a pathological condition (such as an addiction to alcohol or heroin); broadly: dependence on the needs of or control by another.[1]

—Merriam-Webster

Codependence, as commonly understood, occurs when one person tries to control the actions of another (in the guise of helping) so that they can feel better about themselves and their relationship with that other person. The codependence model is rooted in discussions of early-life trauma and the ways in which that can affect later-life behaviors and relationships. Unfortunately, for many loved ones of addicts (and plenty of therapists), framing a person's commitment to helping a troubled loved one as an expression of their own pathology, feels negative, as if they are being blamed, shamed, and pejoratively labeled for loving too much, or not in the right way, or for selfish reasons.

This was likely not the original intent of the codependence movement, but it's what we've currently got. The movement's progenitors were almost certainly not intending to imply that loved ones of addicts provide care based solely on their personal insecurities and neuroses. They did, however, notice that many people in meaningful relationships with an addict had their own chaotic and traumatic pasts. And this observation was carried forward as a primary tenet of the codependence model. As a result, many loving caregivers ended up feeling more blamed, shamed, and defensive than supported.

## THE INCEPTION OF CODEPENDENCE

The pop culture term *codependence* did not come into vogue until the 1980s, but its foundation took root several decades earlier. The true beginnings likely occurred in 1941 with German-born psychoanalyst Karen Horney's theory of the "moving toward" personality style, where one person subconsciously tries to control another through seemingly unselfish, virtuous, faithful, and martyr-like behavior.[2]

A decade later, in 1951, a support group for loved ones of alcoholics, Al-Anon, was founded, recognizing, among other things, the role of "moving toward" behaviors in perpetuating the disease of addiction.[3] Al-Anon addressed, for the first time, the flip side of the alcoholism equation: the pain experienced by the long-suffering spouses and families of alcoholics—the struggles of the people who felt overwhelmed by, at the mercy of, and obsessed with managing their loved one's drinking.

By the 1970s, therapists and drug and alcohol treatment centers embraced Al-Anon, recognizing that addictions affect not only the addict but the addict's family, thus their need for peer support. In 1979, *Newsweek* published an article by Dr. Claudia Black, Dr. Stephanie Brown, and Sharon Wegscheider (now Wegscheider-Cruse) about adult children of alcoholics, introducing to the public the idea that alcoholism in a family can and does cause lifelong patterns of dysfunctional behavior for all members of the family, even those who never take a drink.[4] With this, popular culture embraced the therapeutic belief in treating the disease of addiction, not just individually but part of a family system, spouses were referred to as co-alcoholic, co-addict, or co-chemically dependent, labels that were eventually consolidated and shortened into the much catchier term codependent.

This new and memorable word codependent thus removed unappealing and unpleasant words such as alcoholic, addict, or chemically dependent from the "co" label. It also extended the reach of codependency to anyone in a perceived overly dependent relationship, with or without addiction being present. The term's originally intended link to another person's active addiction(s) was lost. Suddenly, you could be a "co" by simply going out of your way to help a friend who needed a ride across town!

Scott Peck, one of the most successful authors of personal development literature of the time then stated: "Allowing yourself to be dependent on another person is the worst possible thing you can do to yourself . . . If you expect another person to make you happy, you'll be endlessly disappointed."

By the late 1980s, primarily with the release of six books, the term codependence and the ideas surrounding it entered the layperson's lexicon.

- Claudia Black wrote, *It Will Never Happen to Me: Children of Alcoholics as Youngsters, Adolescents, Adults* in 1981.[5]
- Janet Woititz wrote *Adult Children of Alcoholics* in 1982.[6]
- Robin Norwood wrote *Women Who Love Too Much: When You Keep Wishing and Hoping He'll Change* in 1985.[7]
- Timmen Cermak wrote *Diagnosing and Treating Co-dependence* in 1986.[8]
- Melody Beattie wrote *Codependent No More: How to Stop Controlling Others and Start Caring for Yourself* in 1986.[9]
- Pia Mellody wrote *Facing Codependence: What It Is, Where It Comes From, How It Sabotages Our Lives* in 1989.[10]

In *Codependent No More*, Beattie identifies and addresses the pseudo-pathology that has long been attached to the codependence model, writing, "Perhaps one reason some professionals call codependency a disease is because many codependents are reacting to an illness such as alcoholism."[11] There is much impact in this statement. First, it indicates that Beattie did not intend for codependency to be a pathology, that she was instead focused on our gaining insight into the partner's and family's experience. Next, it shows she likely realized, right from the start, that a lot of people would nonetheless view codependence as pathology. So, even before codependence became a thing in the collective mindset, Beattie sensed it would be tied to the disease model of addiction, in particular the belief that addiction is a family illness.

Dr. Cermak, without evidence, espoused this opinion rather forcefully, even proposing an official DSM-based psychiatric diagnosis for codependence as something we today refer to as a chronic personality disorder. Cermak's suggested criteria included behaviors such as:

- Enmeshment in relationships with other psychologically unhealthy people.
- Boundary distortions around intimacy.
- Meeting other people's needs to the exclusion of one's own needs.
- Tying one's self-esteem to validation and support from others.
- Anxiety and hypervigilance about relationships and potential separation.
- Ongoing depression and anxiety.
- Denial of situational reality.
- Their own extensive trauma history.[12]

## TREATMENT CONCEPTS MUST BE PROVEN BEFORE BEING ADOPTED

To accurately evaluate a client's needs and ethically provide effective treatment, therapists are ethically required to utilize validated, universally accepted concepts and language. Having emotional and fact-based insights into a patient's suffering and healing lies at the core of the work. It is the job of the clinical professional to work within the context of such research-based evaluations and treatment methods, adapting them as the therapeutic relationship progresses. Over time, these diagnoses and related treatments may shift as the professional closely observes and responds to the client's progress or lack of. Skillful and effective psychological, psychiatric, and addiction counseling evolves in sync with a therapist's knowledge of their client along with their insight into evolving new methods of care.

I often hear from therapists that they are unquestionably not fans of labeling people. They tell me that us humans are complex, unique beings who will never truly fit into any single category. Still, despite personal beliefs and often-shared frustrations regarding diagnostic tools such as the DSM and ICD (our universal guides to determining mental health diagnoses), we have an unquestionable need for them. Like them or not, these texts offer commonly accepted validated criteria and terminology that provides a shared foundation from which we provide effective care. Without a commonality of how we view our clients' issues and most useful treatments, we would be left to guess how to provide accurate treatment planning, documentation, and clinical work. In other words . . . we need diagnoses to effectively perform our jobs.

## CODEPENDENCY HAS NEVER BEEN A DIAGNOSIS!

If you google codependence or read any of the nearly 400-plus related self-help-books on the topic, you will uncover endless lists delineating the core traits and most useful treatments for codependent people. Alongside this, there are literally hundreds of self-help related quizzes for the consumption of the general public. But when it comes to a formal addiction or mental health diagnosis for codependency, it simply does not exist and it never has.

To this point:

- There has been no formal, validated research on the topic of codependency since 1994.
- Codependency has never been included as a criteria-based diagnosis in the DSM, our sole North American manual of mental health diagnoses.

- Codependency has never been included as a criteria-based diagnosis in the ICD, our sole international manual of mental health diagnoses utilized outside of North America.
- Codependency has never been acknowledged or universally accepted as a formal mental health or addiction assessment tool or diagnosis—not ever.
- Codependency has never been formally accepted by any validated mental health or addiction manuals anywhere in the world.
- As there is no diagnosis, we cannot bill insurance companies for codependency treatment.
- As treatment providers, we put our own credibility at risk when we define a diagnosis and build related treatment plans around a concept that has never been formally defined or accepted.

For nearly four decades, we have been treating troubled and overwhelmed loved ones of addicts as if codependency were a widely validated and legitimate diagnosis. But that is not true. In fact, it has never been true. Perhaps it's time to retire codependence in the museum of past trendy self-help ideas like Bataka bats, primal scream therapy, encounter groups, and rebirthing. As popular as some of these concepts were in their day, in the twenty-first century they would be more accurately placed within the realm of DIY self-help than in expert clinical care. Exciting, new, and popular at the time? Yes. Effective? Not really. The reasons such techniques have not been integrated into formal clinical care is simply because *they have never been proven to work.* That said, we do continue to uncover new, viable, and effective theories and practices. EMDR (eye movement desensitization and reprocessing) represents one such example. When introduced this concept seemed more oddball than anything else, but it has actually turned out to be effective toward easing the pain of working through past trauma. Equally important, is the fact that EMDR has a large amount of validated research to back that up.

In truth, codependency represents one in a long line of hugely fashionable new ideas that entered the therapy space out of pop culture, yet lack validity or proof of their effectiveness. This is the kind of thing that happens when trend-driven concepts become culturally dominant and entrenched in therapeutic care before we have fully evaluated their worth. Science matters. And while good therapy often stems from what feels right to the therapist, accurate diagnoses and related treatment cannot be determined by what feels applicable in the moment. Codependency suggests that professionals (and others) predetermine someone's problems or needs based near solely on that person's circumstances, even before we know them! Legitimate diagnoses and related treatment methods are created and confirmed by the best facts and information that are repeatedly proven over time and then applied on a case-by-case basis:

> It was actually the families of alcoholics and other chemically dependent people who brought the concept of codependency to the attention of therapists in treatment centers. These family members all seemed to be plagued with intensified feelings of shame, fear, anger, and pain in their relationships with the alcoholic or addict who was the focal point of their family. But they often were not able to express these feelings in a healthy way because of a compulsion to please and care for the addicted person. . . .
>
> One irrational aspect was that most of the family members had a deluded hope that if they could only be perfect in their "relating to" and "helping" the alcoholic, they would become sober—and they, the family members, would be free of their awful shame, pain, fear, and anger.[13]

This statement recognizes and summarizes the feelings that many people say they experience when dealing with the addict they love. Their grief and fear mistakenly lead them to think, "If I had effectively controlled the other person's addiction, then everything would have turned out okay." This is their remorse.

## IS CODEPENDENCY A THING?

Right from the start, codependence was conflated with a long-established psychological disorder, Dependent Personality Disorder (DPD). DPD is characterized by "a pervasive and excessive need to be taken care of that leads to submissive and clinging behavior and fears of separation, beginning by early adulthood and present in a variety of contexts."[14] For a DPD diagnosis, individuals must display five or more of the following criteria:

- Difficulty making everyday decisions without an excessive amount of advice and reassurance.
- Needing others to assume responsibility for most major areas of life.
- Difficulty expressing disagreement (based on fear of rejection and loss of support).
- Difficulty initiating projects or doing things on one's own.
- Going to excessive lengths to obtain nurturance and support from others, to the point of volunteering to do things that are unpleasant.
- Feeling uncomfortable or helpless when alone.
- Urgently seeking a new relationship as a source of care and support when one relationship ends.
- An unrealistic preoccupation with the fear of being left alone to take care of oneself.[15]

Ultimately, the proposed codependency diagnosis was rejected. The American Psychiatric Association (APA) felt that people who use enmeshment and attempts to influence or control the behavior of others to an extreme had already been identified by the DPD diagnosis. Therefore, why have a new name for something that already existed?

## CODEPENDENCE GONE AWRY

Unfortunately, the concept of codependence quickly morphed in the minds of the public and a large segment of the therapeutic community, into an unofficial pathology that sounds a lot like a personality disorder, rather than a healthy response to an interpersonal crisis. This morphed viewpoint is now so pervasive that if you go to the Wikipedia page for dependent personality disorder and scroll to the "See Also" section at the bottom, the first hyperlink is to Wikipedia's page on codependency—tangible evidence of how closely aligned the two terms have become in the public mind.[16]

Beattie, perhaps inadvertently, fed this belief in *Codependent No More*, writing:

> When a codependent discontinued his or her relationship with a troubled person, the codependent frequently sought another troubled person and repeated the codependent behaviors with that new person. These behaviors, or coping mechanisms, seemed to prevail throughout the codependent's life—if that person didn't change these behaviors.[17]

Intentionally or otherwise, codependency applied a pathological veneer to those who love and care for addicts. It's like the world woke up one day and decided that displays of inherently powerful strengths of compassion, empathy, and caregiving were somehow a step backward. And based on that set of beliefs we were taught, through the language of codependence, that by letting someone else's needs guide your goals and actions makes you weak and unlikely to meet your own life goals.

That's not codependence. It's anti-dependence.

As stated, this was likely not the intention of the codependency movement's progenitors. Nevertheless, caring for an addicted loved one slowly but steadily continue to be pathologized.

Nowadays, people labeled as codependent are often treated as if they have dependent personality disorder, even when their behavior does not approach that level of pathological neediness and enmeshment. Ross Rosenberg, author of *The Human Magnet Syndrome*,[18] discusses this unfortunate transition in a Psych Central article:

> Like other misunderstood and misused psychological expressions, "codependency" has taken on a life of its own. Once it went mainstream, it was haphazardly and conveniently reshaped to fit our mainstream vocabulary. Since its introduction in the 1980s, its meaning has devolved to describe a weak, needy, clingy, and even emotionally sick person.[19]

Rosenberg's statement may seem harsh, but it's absolutely on target. Codependence has evolved into a belief system that says caring for and trying to help another person, especially if that person is addicted, is an unhealthy, dysfunctional, possibly pathological behavior. Consider the following statement by counselor Scott Egleston, as quoted in *Codependent No More*: "Codependents are caretakers—rescuers. They rescue, then they persecute, then they end up victimized."[20]

About this cycle of codependency-drama interaction, Beattie says:

> We rescue "victims"—people who we believe are not capable of being responsible for themselves. After we rescue, we will inevitably move to

the next corner of the triangle: persecution. We become resentful and angry at the person we have so generously "helped." Then it's time for our final move. We head right for our favorite spot: the victim corner on the bottom. This is the predictable and unavoidable result of a rescue. Feelings of helplessness, hurt, sorrow, shame, and self-pity abound. We have been used—again. We have gone unappreciated—again. We wonder, shall we forever be victims? Probably, if we don't stop rescuing.[21]

According to the codependence model, the answer to one's problems with an addict is to stop rescuing and stop trying to "fix" troubled people. No rescue, no drama. If loved ones of addicts will just look within themselves to identify their own unresolved trauma, they will stop putting others first and eliminate all that drama. Or so says codependency.

To this end, spouses, parents, siblings, and friends of addicts are routinely counseled to accept their own trauma-based weakness, to step away from their dysfunctional relationships, to stop enabling, to stop being so enmeshed, i.e., to "stop being so codependent." Unfortunately, this approach does not empathetically meet such people where they are (anxious, fearful, angry, etc.). This has increasing numbers of people negatively responding to these suggestions, thinking and saying things such as, "How can I possibly abandon a person I love, especially in their hour of deepest need?" Or "How could I be the problem when I have been the functional one all along?"

And therein lies another problem with the codependency model. It inherently prejudges loving, relationally committed people as troubled, near solely based on their life circumstances and choices.

And then, based on that prejudgment, it tells them what to do in order to "get better." As a result, confused, overwhelmed, needful loved ones of addicts take away messages such as:

- I am an active part of the problem.
- I am addicted to the addict.
- Caring for my addicted loved one has made things worse.
- I am broken and defective and unworthy of a healthier relationship.
- I should have seen this coming.
- I don't know how to love someone in a healthy way.
- The ways I love and express my love are creating problems.

Still, family members, friends, pastors, and, yes, even well-educated therapists will work to convince a person that their loving (or raging) attempts to help an addict is a sign of their own dysfunction. Most often, these well-intended advisors suggest therapy, workshops, interventions, and participation in support groups such as CoDA. In this way, they can find support for moving away from what they are told is a bad situation that they are making worse. This viewpoint is required, says codependence, because such problems both distract them from their own life goals and personal fulfillment while simultaneously keeping the addict mired in the problem.

But what are these assessments based upon?

If you google codependence, you'll find dozens of lists delineating the core traits of codependent people, several psychological assessments for codependence, and a variety of self-tests for deciding whether you or someone you know is codependent. These resources range from the ACoA's Laundry List to CoDA's Patterns and Characteristics of Codependence to Charles Whitfield's thirty-eight item Likert-style checklist to the Spann-Fischer Codependency Scale to countless quizzes, lists, and tests provided in blogs, articles, and books on codependence. Regardless of the source, the criteria for codependence inevitably boils down to the following:

- A codependent person makes extreme sacrifices to satisfy the needs of a loved one.
- A codependent person finds it difficult to say no when a loved one makes demands on their time and energy.
- A codependent person covers or tries to manage a loved one's problems with alcohol, drugs, money, the law, etc.
- A codependent person sublimates their needs to meet the needs of loved ones.
- A codependent person is overly focused (to the point of obsession) on the well-being of their troubled loved ones.
- A codependent person has poor boundaries, often doing for addicts (and others) things that they should be doing for themselves.

People who behave in these ways, especially if a loved one is addicted or similarly troubled, tend to be "diagnosed" as codependent. When you take some time to think about it, these traits seem less like a pathology and more like a person who cares deeply about the well-being of a troubled loved one.

Ask yourself:

- Who doesn't make sacrifices for a person they love, especially if that person is struggling?
- Who doesn't say yes to a family member asking for assistance?
- Who doesn't help someone they love who is in desperate straits?
- Who doesn't try to help their family save face in difficult circumstances?
- Who wouldn't sublimate their needs to help a struggling loved one who may die if you do not?

- Who doesn't worry obsessively when a loved one is struggling and ill?
- Who hasn't overstepped healthy boundaries at least occasionally in a misguided but well-meaning attempt to help a loved one?

## CODEPENDENCY IS GENDER BIASED

Therapeutic errors based on being human are to be expected, but institutionalized treatment methods that are awash in sex or gender bias are never acceptable. Consider how the therapy and counseling fields today view the treatment needs of homosexual and transgender clients versus the methods employed in the 1970s and 1980s. Such profound changes in therapy have evolved in direct relationship to over a century of shifting social norms combined with more objective research. In the past, flawed research into these populations arose out of biased cultural beliefs about homosexuality, bisexuality, sexual fetishism, and trans-sexuality. This information, at the time reinforced by existing societal norms, pushed us to provide forms of care that today are considered unethical. What we understood to be correct forty to fifty years ago simply isn't. In the twenty-first century, we no longer view variations in gender expression, sexual orientation and gender identity as pathologies needing to be eliminated. In fact, today we view professionals and clergy who continue to practice in these ways as offensive as such approaches have been proven to cause more harm than good.

This brings us back (again) to codependency.

As stated above, feminist ideas that filtered down into the therapy world via codependency suggest that women who demonstrate meaningful empathy, compassion, and dependency (especially toward men) are inherently troubled because they have prioritized caring for others over a primary focus on themselves. As Janice Haaken stated in 1990, "The codependency literature focuses almost exclusively on pathology, basing itself on a deficit rather than a strength-based model of women's personalities." These concepts simply do not leave room for women to lead with empathy *and* assertiveness; they have to choose one or the other. And codependency, with its strong messages of individuation, self-reliance, and anti-dependency (from men), serves to reinforce these beliefs.

In their study of the relationships between codependency and masculinity and femininity, George Dear and Claire Roberts state that "the gender-role measures that showed the greatest association with codependency were the socially undesirable aspects of femininity and the socially desirable aspects of masculinity." Similarly, in their study of codependency and gender-stereotyped traits, Gloria Cowan and Lynda Warren concluded that the essence of codependency is a failure to conform to "the cultural definition of the healthy man."[22]

In the 1970s and 1980s, when codependency was in its nascency, this new form of "pathology" (over-dependence on or enmeshment with others) was not focused toward, nor did it relate to the experience of most men. After all, men already had authority, power, and hundreds of years of deference to male decision-making on their side. Men weren't watching films like *9 to 5* (the story about women fighting back against male domination in the workplace mentioned earlier). Men were watching movies like *Top Gun* that served to support and validate their sense of power. As Anne Wilson Schaef stated in 1986, "Although men can theoretically be codependent, all the literature refers almost exclusively to women as having the disease."[23] From the mid-1980s to this day, when a woman expresses deep empathy, love, and ongoing commitment toward an addicted or otherwise troubled man, she is likely to be viewed as part of the problem rather than part of the solution.

From the mid-1980s to this day, when a woman expresses deep empathy, love, and ongoing commitment toward an addicted or otherwise troubled man, she is likely to be viewed as part of the problem rather than part of the solution.

Sadly, the concept of codependency embraces this bias *against women by women* with its incessant message that being deeply, unabashedly and mutually interdependent (as are all healthy humans) means giving away your personal power. In this way, codependency fails to validate our natural and powerful desire (and typically feminine strength) to compassionately support and help those they love, especially when they are in trouble.

## CODEPENDENCY IS CULTURALLY BIASED

The basic building blocks of all proven and effective therapy and counseling methods must be applicable *across cultures.* We don't abandon successful models of therapy and support related to differing cultures, we build upon them, and we adapt them—*provided they are adaptable.* Adapting our work means choosing the most effective forms of care that also reflect each person's cultural background and experiences. In one example, clients whose lives are deeply rooted in Christian religious beliefs can feel mistrusting of therapy that lacks an integration of biblical scripture. When working with such clients, we need to interweave validated, useful therapy methods with our client's deeply held religious beliefs or we need to refer them out to someone who can. This point reinforces the previously stated concept that the method chosen to help someone must be adapted to meet

that person *where that person is*. We can pick any model of supportive help we know to be effective with the issues presented, and then
it's our job to make those concepts applicable. However, this is only
possible by utilizing therapy modalities that are universally adaptable.
Eurocentric treatment models like codependency are, by definition,
grounded in concepts of personal development, self-actualization,
and individuation rather than dependence on family and collective
community bonds. Thus, the codependency model at its core is inap-
plicable when applied to families, ethnicities, cultures, and religions
that inherently value community-sourced healing over self-reliance.
Reflecting this challenge to the treatment process, therapist and soci-
ologist Marianne Diaz states:

> As we know, acculturation has been a problem for people of color in
> America. For example, a lot of therapeutic processes and theories that
> Latinx clients get exposed to, amount to their being told that they have to
> "find time for themselves" or "initiate more self-care"—in other words,
> to individuate. This does not really resonate with the Latinx population
> as we are a culture about the collective. So when you start hearing a
> clinician say—and it's not intentional, it's just what they know—"make
> time for yourself, you need not worry so much about the family," that
> in itself has people in my community thinking, "You don't get me and
> my culture." Because in the Latinx culture, thinking that way makes you
> selfish.[24]

As the primary goals of codependency are unquestionably rooted
in concepts of personal growth and self-reliance over community, the
model cannot be defined as cross-cultural. Any therapeutic concepts
that skews heavily toward individual healing over leaning into the
collective for support is anathema to most Native American, African
American, Asian, and Hispanic cultures—to name just a few. For

such people, a focus on personal growth over shared connections can be viewed as self-centered and in direct conflict with deeply held community-focused values. In this way, codependency fails to meet the standards for a cross-cultural model of treatment.

## CODEPENDENCY IS ANTI-DEPENDENT

One of the defining hypotheses underlying this book is the belief that codependency is anti-dependent rather than interdependent. To this point, we need look no further than Beattie's *Codependent No More* where she wrote the following:

> "Stop seeking so much approval and validation from others, we don't need the approval of everyone and anyone, we only need our own approval. We have all the same sources for happiness and making choices inside of us that others do, so find and develop your own internal supply of peace, well-being and self-esteem. *Relationships help, but they cannot be our source.*" [Emphasis added.]

In the twenty-first century, such strong messages of self-actualization via independence no longer define our view of mental health. For the most part, such views have been replaced by relationship-focused beliefs about human fulfillment and contentment.

## WHEN COUNSELORS DO MORE HARM THAN GOOD

Michelle is the forty-eight-year-old wife of Alex, an active alcoholic. The couple has three children, ages eleven, fourteen, and twenty-one. For years, Michelle has covered up and attempted to manage Alex's drinking with varying degrees of success. Now her eldest child, Jonathan, is abusing drugs and has dropped out of college. Michelle is perpetually worried that Alex will get fired for missing too much work as he often skips out to drink or shows up at his job drunk. Meanwhile, her son Jonathan is living in a crowded two-bedroom apartment with four other dropouts, supporting himself with a part-time, minimum-wage job and a steady stream of "loans" from his parents. For now, the younger children seem to be doing okay in school and socially, but Michelle worries they will follow in their older brother's footsteps or worse.

Unsure about how she should handle everything that she and her loved ones are going through, and terrified about her family's future, Michelle finally seeks therapy desperately seeking direction toward healing her family. After listening to Michelle's gut-wrenching, tearful, and angry story of what is happening in her life, her highly recommended addiction-trained therapist offers a bit of emotional support. Following that she simply does what she's been taught, which is to turn to a disease model for treating loved ones of addicts called codependence.

Over the next several weeks, this well-meaning professional focuses treatment on Michelle's underlying trauma, trying to help her understand that her inadequate childhood has led her into a codependent relationship. It is also suggested that she and her addicted husband are reenacting their own dysfunctional histories with their kids in a form of generational illness. She can already see this occurring with Jonathan's addiction and is told that this is going to get worse unless she gains much needed insight into her own troubled history.

This frustrates Michelle, who simply seeks validation for her fears, appreciation for her giving and caretaking, direction on what comes next, and, most of all, hope. This seemingly endless therapy focused on her early-life trauma and the damage it has wrought leaves her feeling alienated and ashamed. And that does not make sense to her. After all, she is not the addict and she is not the problem.

Feeling unheard and misunderstood by her therapist, she often has angry outbursts during her sessions. Unfortunately, as her frustration mounts, her therapist leans more heavily into the codependence model. And why not? After all, the therapist is trained to understand that Michelle's anger and pain are derived from her own trauma and her unwillingness to accept that she is codependent.

And let's face it, no therapist likes an angry client who screams, yells, cries, blames others, and won't take responsibility. It's so much easier to have Michelle focus on herself as the primary source of all that loss, anger, and regret. In this way, codependency allows the counselor to take all of Michelle's pain and fear and put a nice label on it, wrap it in a bow, and give it back to her as the source of her underlying unhappiness.

## WHAT'S WRONG HERE?

What typically does not work in these kinds of situations is telling loved ones of addicts that their desire to caretake is a manifestation of their own disease. Nevertheless, many caregiving loved ones will (grudgingly) accept the codependence label, tacitly agreeing to themselves be pathologized. After all, it's not like they are not shown or offered any alternative approaches. Despite the fact that codependency has led to the addictive mirror being turned on them, they are nonetheless willing to do whatever is necessary to help their family heal. And they will do so even if that means sacrificing their own reality. In recent days, increasing numbers of caregivers simply walk away from treatment that they desperately need because they don't believe they are being accurately heard or understood. At worst, they feel insulted and judged; at best they feel that what is being offered doesn't apply. As a result, they don't get the care and guidance they so desperately need. And this is what happened to Michelle. She stuck it out for about two months, felt like she was getting nowhere, and decided to exit therapy. In the end, there was no useful help for Michelle, no useful help for Alex or Jonathan, and no useful help for their young children. All Michelle got from this experience was a sense of being labeled, blamed, and misunderstood.

## HOW IS THIS HELPFUL?

Sadly, we hear stories like Michelle's far too often. The caregiving loved one of an addict being overwhelmed, and fearful, seeks therapeutic validation, support, and guidance on how to make things better. But instead of receiving warm, empathetic support, they are told that they, too, must change as their unacknowledged trauma has led to their codependence. How does a message like this meet anyone's emotional needs? Michelle is hurt, fearful, and needs validation for what she is feeling and doing. She needs guidance about how to more productively take better care of herself while also loving and caring for her addicted loved ones. She needs others to understand that she has exhausted herself trying to "keep it all together" for the sake of her family. She needs those who support her and especially her therapist to understand and affirm that she has done all of this out of her love for her family.

Instead of treating the loved ones of addicts as if they also have a pathology, why not find more compassion within ourselves and recognize them as loving, caring, connection-oriented individuals in crisis? That is what prodependence is all about.

## Prodependence in Action

*What if Michelle had encountered a therapist who viewed her issues through a prodependence lens? How would her experience have differed from the one described earlier? From a prodependent perspective, it might look like a bit like this.*

Michelle enters counseling overwhelmed and exhausted from trying to keep her family together. Her husband is broken and unavailable despite her attempts to help him, and her kids are now beginning their own personal journey into dysfunction. All of this leaves her feeling increasingly helpless and somehow at fault.

The professional assigned to help Michelle greets her with open arms, gratefully acknowledging her devotion and sacrifice. "How kind you have been," she tells Michelle, "to have given so much of yourself to those you love. What a gift you are to them." Then, recognizing Michelle's exhaustion and feelings of despair, the therapist says, "You must be so worn out now, and who wouldn't be in your situation? And despite your best efforts things are still slowly but steadily getting worse. I bet you're worried that somehow you haven't given enough."

Michelle nods and sobs with tears of validation.

After a moment, the therapist says, "You undoubtedly need more support for the good fight you are in to fix your family. After all, how could anyone solve all these problems on their own no matter how much love they have in their heart?

Why don't we work together to see if we can relieve some of your burdens, while at the same time finding the best possible path toward healing your family? Does that sound good?

Prodependence suggests there are no long looks into anyone's past; neither Michelle's nor the families, therefore:

- There is no mention of dysfunction or problems with Michelle or her caregiving (except that she might be overwhelmed and need help).
- There is no criticism of what Michelle has done or challenges to the way she has done it.
- There is no suggestion of Michelle being "part of the problem."
- She is greeted with validation, compassion, and empathy.

By leading with this model, the professional readily and quickly earns Michelle's trust, helping her feel both understood and supported. And it is from this place of mutual respect and empathy that a path can be made to help Michelle engage in much-needed self-care and set healthy boundaries with her family, all the while working to build an empathetic community of support.

Now, you tell me, in which treatment scenario will Michelle feel more valued, validated, and motivated. If you said prodependence, then you're beginning to understand the power of love in action. Instead of being blamed and considered as part of the problem, here Michelle is validated for her strength, love, and devotion, and because she is committed to doing whatever it takes to help those she loves.

# Chapter Five

# OUR NEED TO CONNECT

*Splendid isolation is for planets, not people.*[1]

—Sue Johnson, *Love Sense*

## BROKEN PEOPLE, NOT BAD PEOPLE

Addicts have traditionally been defined as a people suffering from moral failing, a lack of self-will, or a deep psychological flaw. This view left no room for an addict to be seen as someone suffering from a chronic form of emotional illness. As stated, these beliefs began to shift in the mid-twentieth century as our understanding and views of addiction began to slowly but steadily evolve toward the disease model that exists today.

Part and parcel with implementation of the disease model was the recognition that addicts are themselves often survivors of severe or early chronic trauma.[2] And the more we learn about addiction, the more sense this makes. It is clear from both research and clinical observation that addictions are not about feeling good, they're about feeling less. Addicts turn to addictive substances and behaviors not to have a good time, but rather to self-medicate and self-regulate. An addict's primary goal is to escape from life and avoid stressors.

> It is clear from both research and clinical observation that addictions are not about feeling good, they're about feeling less. Addicts turn to addictive substances and behaviors not to have a good time, but rather to self-medicate and self-regulate. An addict's primary goal is to escape from life and avoid stressors.

And don't kid yourself, addictions work if the goal is to escape reality as addictive substances and behaviors trigger a highly distracting neurochemical response. This occurs as the addicted brain—when entering an addictive cycle—begins to release dopamine (pleasure), along with adrenaline (excitement), oxytocin (love and connection), serotonin (emotional well-being), and a variety of endorphins (euphoria). This response evokes sensations of pleasure, excitement, control, and most importantly, distraction via emotional and psychological disassociation.

Most addicts abuse addictive substances and behaviors and continue to do so even as their out-of-control behaviors create significant problems: relationship issues, trouble at work or in school, declining physical and/or emotional health, financial turmoil, legal concerns, mood disorders, and more. Addicts cope with stress, depression, anxiety, loneliness, boredom, enthusiasm, and unresolved trauma by getting high or behaviorally acting out rather than gaining emotional support from healthy relationships with trusted people. As they do this repeatedly, choices become habits and habits become addictions. Gabor Maté writes in his bestselling book, *In the Realm of Hungry*

*Ghosts,* "It is impossible to understand addiction without asking what relief the addict finds, or hopes to find, in the drug or the addictive behavior."[3]

## HUMANS ARE PACK ANIMALS

Human beings are inherently designed to work together, not to go it alone. To reinforce this concept, think about the prehistoric times when people lived in tribes. If we went hunting, we went in a group; otherwise, we were as likely to be eaten as to eat. As hunting trips could take a very long time, other members of the tribe stayed behind to tan the animal hides used to keep the group warm, gathered nuts and berries to eat, and helped oversee and manage children and elders, all the while working together to keep their community safe.

For thousands of years, this type of communal living was how we survived. Because of this, our brains evolved in ways that encourage interpersonal bonding and attachment, rather than going it alone (detachment.) We are evolutionarily wired to be dependent upon others. We enter the world completely reliant on other people for shelter, nutrition, and emotional support (love), and these core requirements do not change as we grow older. What keeps us healthy as children also keeps us healthy as adults. Even in late adolescence, when we tend to individuate from our families, we don't move toward isolation. Instead, our dependence needs shift from parents and family to peers and eventually creating families of our own.

Yet somehow, as we move into adulthood, our intrinsic need for emotional connection has been discounted. This despite the fact that people who spend their lives "apart from" rather than "a part of " do not function as well as those who feel emotionally connected.

Nearly all of our current research shows that isolated/separated individuals are more likely to suffer both emotionally and physically.[4] Conversely, people who place a high value on developing and maintaining meaningful social and familial connections tend to be happier, more resilient, and more successful.[5] They even tend to live longer.[6] Thus we see that emotionally intimate connections are nearly as essential to life and well-being as are food, water, and shelter.

> Lacking connection, we may survive, but we won't be happy. When we go it alone, we fail to thrive. And our deeply ingrained need for emotional connection does not abate because a person we love, with whom we feel an intimate bond, is challenged by an addiction or some other serious problem.

Lacking connection, we may survive, but we won't be happy. When we go it alone, we fail to thrive. And our deeply ingrained need for emotional connection does not abate because a person we love, with whom we feel an intimate bond, is challenged by an addiction or some other serious problem.

Dr Marion Solomon states the following:

> Dependency is not immaturity, an unhealthy sign of regression, or a sign of pathology. Positive dependency allows you to maintain close bonds, to feel open and connected to experience yourself as enhanced within the context of something larger, a relationship, a community, a family in which you take pride.[7]

## ATTACHMENT AND EMOTIONAL WELL-BEING

Attachment theory was developed as a psychological construct in the 1940s and 1950s by psychologist John Bowlby. In formulating his theories, Bowlby first studied WWII orphans in Europe, finding that even though these children received adequate food, shelter, and physical care, they did not seem to thrive like normal children. Some of them developed so poorly that they died.[8] This is a concept we now call infantile depression or failure to thrive. Bowlby theorized that the development of emotional bonds might be an evolutionary survival mechanism. Basically, Bowlby felt that wanting and needing a constant and reliable source of love and support has evolved into a survival mechanism, every bit as crucial to the existence and success of human beings as opposable thumbs. In the beginning, Bowlby's theories were almost universally dismissed. (Keep in mind, this was the Dr. Spock era when coddling children was discouraged because it was seen as being counterproductive to their long-term well-being.[9]) Nevertheless, after watching so many orphans fail to thrive and at times fail to survive, even though nothing appeared physically wrong with them, Bowlby kept at it. Eventually, he hired a brilliant Canadian researcher named Mary Ainsworth as his assistant and colleague. It was Ainsworth who devised the breakthrough study, codifying the four behaviors that she and Bowlby saw as essential to healthy attachment:

1) We must monitor and maintain physical closeness with our loved one(s) and caregiver(s).
2) We reach out to our loved one(s) and caregiver(s) when upset.
3) We miss our loved one(s) and caregiver(s) when we are apart.
4) We count on our loved one(s) and caregiver(s) to be there for us in order to go out into the world.

Ainsworth is famous for a study called The Strange Situation.[10] In this experiment, Ainsworth and Bowlby put a child and his mother in a room filled with toys and other interesting items, and the mother was instructed to let the child explore the room. After a few minutes, a stranger entered the room and chatted with the mother. Then the stranger turned their attention to the child, while the mother left the room. After several minutes, the mother returned to interact with her child, comforting the child if necessary. Then the mother and the stranger both left the room. After a few minutes alone, the mother was sent back into the room to be with her child.

Unsurprisingly, the young children were almost always visibly upset when their mother left them with a stranger or completely alone—crying, throwing toys, rocking themselves, etc. Some, however, were less upset than others. They calmed themselves quickly, and they reconnected easily with their mother when she returned. These "emotionally resilient" children seemed confident that their mothers would be there when they really wanted and needed them. Meanwhile, the less emotionally resilient children displayed greater degrees of upset when their mother left the room, and greater difficulty reconnecting with her when she returned. They were less confident that she would be there when they needed her.

Notably, Ainsworth and Bowlby noticed that the more easygoing kids had visibly warmer and more emotionally responsive mothers, while the more anxious kids had cooler and less responsive mothers. With this observation, the researchers felt they'd witnessed the power of love in action.

Slowly but steadily, other researchers joined the attachment theory bandwagon. Psychologist Harry Harlow experimented using rhesus monkeys separated from their mothers at birth. He found that the isolated underfed infant monkeys were so hungry for emotional connection that when given a choice between a "mother" made of wire who dispensed food and a soft-cloth mother without food, they invariably chose the squashy rag mother.[11] Harlow also found that these motherless monkeys matured physically but not emotionally. As adults, they failed to understand the social cues of other monkeys, they displayed signs of depression, they were self-destructive, they failed to develop normal problem-solving skills, and they were unable to mate.

We see similar results in us humans. Those who do not securely attach as infants and small children tend to become more readily depressed, anxious, self-destructive, and emotionally isolated as adults. That is a sad fact but undeniably true. Without a doubt, many people have wonderfully healthy childhoods, and, because of that, they learn to attach securely and healthfully. But many others do not. And I'll bet you can accurately guess which group is more likely to deal with addiction, as either an addict or the loved one of an addict.

## About Attachment Styles

Adult attachment styles generally refer to the way in which individuals feel and behave toward intimacy within the context of their primary relationships. Levine and Heller (2019) point out that understanding the three attachment styles (secure, anxious, and avoidant)—or a combination of them—can assist a therapist in predicting behavior in romantic situations. Although the prodependence model is heavily based on attachment theories, specifically regarding human connections taking place when addiction is present, it does not focus on attachment styles. Our discussions of attachment used throughout this book refer to the human neurobiological propensity for intimate and secure human bonding. A foundational belief of codependence is those who remain by the side of an active addict do so because they are working out their own issues. A foundational, interdependent belief of prodependence is those who remain by the side of an active addict do so because they are deeply and meaningfully attached to that person.

## SECURE ATTACHMENT

The most effective caregivers are ones who are consistently responsive to the day-to-day needs of their children, which leads to greater self-esteem and emotional stability in adult life. Such caregivers do this by providing a secure base from which the child can comfortably depart, wander, explore, and learn, and then return for nurturing, love, and comfort. In this way, they learn and internalize the life lesson that others can be relied upon for support, nurturance, and soothing.

Early in life, a child's forays away from their secure base are usually brief. As the child grows, these excursions tend to go farther and last longer. Eventually, if managed consistently and with care, the child grows into a separate yet connected person who has internalized a sense of security and stability. Because the child has a secure base, they tend to be more internally confident and comfortable around others. Over time, the more structure, consistency and nurturing a child experiences, the more they are led to becoming an adult who can innately provide their own internal emotional regulation. The securely attached child learns that a healthy response from their caregiver(s) is the norm. The child fully believes that support will consistently be there when they need it. The child is secure in this belief and trusts in the goodness and health of the attachment that they have developed with family and others.

Our early learned experience of basic trust then extends into adult life and adult relationships. We natively trust and rely on other people until proven otherwise—importantly we come to trust our own instincts and emotions.

Unfortunately, early-life caregivers who are absent, impaired, addicted, neglectful, anxious, inconsistent, intrusive, mentally ill, narcissistic, overbearing, or similarly unreliable, teach their young that asking for their dependency needs to be met does not lead to feeling secure, but rather that it can be both threatening and dangerous. And this makes so much sense, as *what could be more painful than loving into a void.* These experiences (more about surviving than thriving), stunt the child's ability to explore the world confidently and to grow in healthy ways. Moreover, the child will tend to feel anxious about self, others, and the world. Moreover, they will tend to feel anxious about themselves and others, leading to an adult life more filled with shame, low self-esteem and insecurity, than pride and relational comfort. Such unfortunate people likely attempt to cope with those fears and insecurities in their adult lives in one or more of the following maladaptive ways:

- Turning to escapist (often addictive) substances and/or behaviors to provide their own self-soothing.
- Avoiding emotional intimacy.
- Difficulty tolerating emotional discomfort and loneliness.
- Repeated attempts to bond (to gain a secure attachment) with people who are unable to meet that need.
- Relying only on themselves and how others respond to them to determine their self-worth.
- Becoming overly controlling toward others and their environment.
- Becoming overly self-sufficient and walled off.

- Failing to trust others even when trust is merited and needed.
- Isolating emotionally and/or physically, often in conjunction with an addiction or other psychological disorder (depression, anxiety, dissociative disorders and the like).

As children we require shelter, nutrition, and emotional support (love) and those needs do not change as we become adults. Admittedly, our need for love and emotional support evolves and looks different as we move from infant to toddler to child to adolescent to young adult to adult. But it does not disappear. And if this need is not met, we suffer. As human beings we have an innate, hardwired need for emotional closeness, and we ignore this requirement at our peril. To survive and thrive, we need food, shelter, and love. Without all these necessities, we tend to struggle—as kids, as teens, and as adults.

## Secure Versus Insecure Attachment

Over the years, numerous models of attachment have been developed, which don't require detailed discussion here. The primary point is that different people attach in different ways. The short version of the discussion boils down to three basic ideas:

1) We tend to attach either securely or insecurely.
2) Our basic attachment style, be it secure or insecure, develops very early in life—mostly during our infant and toddler years.
3) Our basic attachment style tends to be relatively stable over our life span.

Simply stated, individuals who experience healthy attachment in childhood, courtesy of responsive caregivers, tend to securely attach as adults. Those who do not experience healthy and reliable attachment in childhood, tend to struggle with attachment as kids and also as adults.

The good news is that our ability and willingness to attach to others is not set in stone. "Earned security" can be achieved by troubled, empty people over time, typically through a combination of therapy and the development and nurturance of empathetic, mutually supportive relationships.

But here's the rub: in order to learn that others can and will respond to your needs, you have to risk and learn how to attach in healthier ways. But this is a tricky and difficult path for many as getting there involves becoming vulnerable (thus risking rejection, abandonment, and everything else that fed into their currently insecure state). As psychobiologist Dr. Stan Tatkin writes, "If we feel insecure about close relationships, there is no way to become more secure without being in one." So, to overcome our fears about attachment, we must face our fears and become attached. And that is not easy. Especially when the world around us views vulnerability and the dependence we inherently crave as undesirable, overly needy traits.

## PERFECTLY IMPERFECT PARENTS

As discussed earlier, infants and toddlers are hardwired to rely on primary caregivers (usually, though not always, their parent) for safety, comfort, and emotional attunement. Young children naturally and innately seek out the secure base of caregivers, especially in times of emotional and/or physical distress, seeking proximity and security. In the ideal world, a child learns over time to trust others, especially loved ones, because those loved ones are appropriately responsive to the child's needs. As a result, the child develops autonomy, feels industrious, cultivates a healthy self-image, believes in themselves and their abilities, loves, achieves, and feels good about the life that they are living. But you don't need a perfect caregiver to get there.

The "good-enough" parent is responsive in healthy and appropriate ways enough of the time that the child learns to trust and develops a secure sense of attachment (or at least a mostly secure sense of attachment), even when the parent is not perfectly responsive all the time. Their imperfection forces the child to grow and to develop in ways that support and encourage self-esteem and self-sufficiency—while still allowing the child to feel (mostly) securely attached.

Interestingly, this same concept holds true in families dealing with addiction. Loved ones of addicts are at their best when they provide relatively consistent and reliable support without being 100 percent caretaker. The best way to care for an addict is to love and support them while encouraging them to grow by living and experiencing their lives (including addiction-related consequences). There is a happy medium for loved ones of addicts. Enmeshment and control are not good for the addict or the family, but neither is detaching with love and just plain walking away, as the codependency model so often suggests. One also has to question the concept of "detachment with love" as it may be more of an oxymoron than an achievable state.

## GOING IT ALONE

Sadly, in modern Western culture, being dependent on others is generally viewed as a sign of weakness. We are taught, almost from birth, regardless of gender, that we're on our own, we shouldn't rely on others, that our success and happiness are completely dependent on us. We grow up learning that independence, self-sufficiency, and making it through life without the assistance of others is the right way and maybe the only path toward self-satisfaction and self-esteem.

This, despite the fact that nearly all of our research tells us the exact opposite by examining what happens to those who allow themselves to be open to healthy consistent connections and dependencies. For example:

- A consistent sense of loneliness can raise blood pressure to the point where the risk of heart attack and stroke doubles.[12]
- Distress in an existing relationship increases the risk of heart problems.[13]
- Distress in an existing relationship increases the risk of problems with the immune and hormonal systems.[14]
- Social isolation and relationship distress have been linked to increased instances of the common cold.[15]
- Social isolation and relationship distress have been linked to lowered odds of surviving a natural disaster.[16]
- The research goes on and on, repeatedly revealing an undeniable link between a lack of connectedness and diminished well-being. One study suggests that this link is every bit as strong and every bit as damning as the link between smoking and poor health.[17]

## IN PERSONAL TERMS

About sixteen years ago, a therapist friend said to me, "You know, ever since you moved in with your partner, you seem more focused, more stable, and even more creative." As lovely as that sounds to me today, back then her offhand comment felt more like criticism than validation. In my mind, based on all I'd been taught, I believed that I should be just as successful and creative when single as when in a relationship. My upbringing was very clear in this regard: An independent man is stronger and better than one who is dependent and therefore weak. My family and culture taught me from day one that a primary life goal is to be self-sufficient, comfortable with independence, and appreciative of time spent alone. Additionally, I was told that the road to relationship happiness was paved by independent hard work and achievement. So, after my friend essentially told me just the opposite, I wondered why she was telling me I seemed better off when in a relationship. Did that mean something was wrong with me?

Looking back on this today—understanding it with the benefit of much hard-won life wisdom—I realize that she was right. Moreover, she was explaining one of the basic building blocks of life in a way I had not previously considered. She wasn't speaking in greeting-card platitudes such as, "Life is better when we're together." Nor was she saying that I was a failure or less of a man because I thrived when in a healthy relationship. She simply recognized that I do better with a loving hand by my side. Today, I see my deep need for ongoing connection as a strength. By recognizing, responding to, and anticipating that need today, I feel I am a better person—and a better man. Today, I am more creative, successful, and more at peace than at any time when I was single.

Research tells us that when we feel securely attached to trusted others, we are healthier, more confident, engage in healthier risk taking, and achieve our life goals faster. So, stated very simply, we do better in all aspects of life when we feel loved and supported. When we feel securely connected, we blossom and grow.

So how can emotional dependence be a weakness?

My friend and colleague, Dr. Sue Johnson, states the matter as succinctly and eloquently as anyone, writing, "Love is not the icing on the cake of life. It is a basic primary need, like oxygen or water."[18] I could not agree more. The Dr. Spock–influenced society of the 1950s got it wrong when he told us that by leaving unhappy children to 'cry it out' they would become stronger as adults. In fact, adults become stronger because they receive consistently responsive attention. Actively and consistently responding to our children in an age-appropriate manner from womb to tomb is the path toward their lifelong happiness. We need to hold one another, we need to care for one another in healthy ways, and we need to overtly express our love and have that love returned on every level. Without this, we suffer, just as we would if we were not eating, sleeping, or keeping a roof over our heads. And this truth does not diminish because we are dealing with a loved one's addiction.

## Chapter Six

# ADDICTION IS AN INTIMACY DISORDER

*Addiction is the only prison where the locks are on the inside.*

—Unknown

## ADDICTION EQUALS ISOLATION

Throughout human history, one of the worst possible forms of punishment was not prison or even death; it was exile. In one such example, in 1814 the controversial military leader, politician, and megalomaniac Napoleon Bonaparte was exiled after ten years as self-proclaimed Emperor of France to the Mediterranean isle of Elba. He was separated from his wife and son, who were sent to Austria. A year later he escaped, returned to France, and retook his throne for approximately one hundred days before his ultimate defeat at Waterloo. As punishment, he was again exiled, this time to a much smaller and more remote island, St. Helena, 1,000 miles from the nearest land mass. Once more, he was sent away without his wife and son. By all accounts, he died a miserable, protracted, and very lonely death on St. Helena.

In the 1800s, you could be drawn and quartered, tortured on the rack, beheaded, hung, and subjected to all sorts of other incredibly nasty punishments. But note that the meanest, most miserable punishment that anyone could think of for Napoleon was exile. And frankly, not much has changed. When people do something wrong in modern society, we send them to prison, a form of exile. And if they misbehave in prison, we put them in solitary confinement, an extra layer of exile.

Addicts don't get this need for ongoing intimate connections. After all they have drugs, alcohol, and addictive behaviors to help them tolerate their self-imposed isolation. Addicts choose to live in emotional exile, and they do not break this exile because they report feeling most alone when in the company of other people. And yes, other people includes spouses, family, and other loved ones.

This fear of connection is learned through neglect, abuse, and other forms of traumatic experiences. Addicts learn to fear and avoid emotional vulnerability and dependency, instead turning to their addiction. When addicts become emotionally needful—related to stress, losses, anxiety, depression, and even joy—they automatically, without conscious thought, turn not outward toward others but rather inward toward their addiction as a controllable source of emotional comfort.

Addicts exile themselves because they learned early on that turning to other people for support, validation, and comfort can leave them feeling worse than before they reached out. Thus, they avoid the type of deep relational connections that, for healthier people, bring needed consolation, emotional resolution, stability, consistency, and reward. In short, addicts use their addiction as a maladaptive distraction from their painfully unmet emotional dependency needs.

Addictions are not moral failings. Addictions are not weaknesses. Addictions are not a lack of moral fiber. Addictions are essentially a form of intimacy disorder that require a lifetime of deliberate connection for them to become and remain sober. Addicts are, for the most part, not malicious people, they are broken people.

When addiction is conceptualized—as an intimacy disorder—we can clearly see that the best treatment for addiction is not the pursuit of sobriety; rather the best treatment for addiction is the pursuit of healthy, intimate, ongoing reliable connections. Thus, a fundamental task of addiction treatment beyond sobriety is to help the addicted person develop and maintain supportive emotional bonds.

> When addiction is conceptualized—as an intimacy disorder—we can clearly see that the best treatment for addiction is not the pursuit of sobriety; rather the best treatment for addiction is the pursuit of healthy, intimate, ongoing reliable connections.

It is this approach—not willpower, or babysitters, or shaming, or threatened consequences—that is most likely to lead to lasting sobriety, emotional healing, and a happier, healthier life.

## ADDICTION THRIVES IN ISOLATION

One of the all-time great illustrations of addiction as an intimacy disorder occurs in Canadian researcher Bruce Alexander's famed "Rat Park" study. Prior to Alexander's work, it was generally believed that pleasure, as wrought by addictive substances and behaviors, was the primary driver of addiction. Bolstering this belief was the fact that most early research on the root causes of addiction centered on the neurochemical pleasure response and the fact that lab rats, when given the choice, would nearly always choose to drink opiate-infused water over regular water. For a long while, even the National Institute on Drug Abuse espoused this "pleasure drives addiction" viewpoint.[1]

However, based solely on the fact that most people do not become addicts (for instance, the Substance Abuse and Mental Health Administration estimates that almost every American adult has tried alcohol, but only about 6.8 percent become alcoholic[2]), it seemed clear to at least a few addiction treatment specialists and researchers that pleasure was not the primary driver of addiction and that the desire for pleasure was not what caused some people (and rats) to return to a potentially addictive substance or behavior over and over, compulsively and to their detriment.

Recognizing this, Alexander reexamined the results of then-existing rat studies, where test subjects were placed in empty cages, alone, with two water bottles to choose from—one with pure water, the other with opiate-infused water. In those experiments, the rats uniformly got hooked on and eventually overdosed on the opiate water, leading researchers to conclude that the out-of-control search for extreme pleasure drives addictions. This led to a belief that addicts were just weak people, and if they could only develop some willpower things would be okay.

## LONELY RATS

Alexander disagreed. He was bothered by the fact that the cages in which lab rats were isolated were small, with no potential for stimulation beyond the opiate water. He thought, "Of course they get high. What else are they supposed to do?" In response, he created the rat park, a cage approximately 200 times larger than the typical isolation cage, with hamster wheels and multicolored balls to play with, plenty of tasty food to eat, and spaces for mating and raising litters.[3] And he put not one rat, but twenty rats (of both genders) into the cage. Then, and only then, did he mirror the old experiments.

And guess what? Alexander's now apparently happy rats ignored the opiate water, expressing much more interest in typical communal rat activities such as playing, fighting, eating, and mating. Even rats who'd previously been isolated and drinking the drugged water left it alone when they were placed in the rat park. With a little bit of social stimulation and connection, addiction in rats disappeared.

An interdependent interpretation of Alexander's experiment versus prior experiments is as follows: Putting a rat in a small cage, alone, is a form of exile. That exile mirrors what some traumatized, insecurely attached human beings do—shut themselves off from intimacy because they did not learn how to create deeply emotional bonds. In such self-imposed human exile, emotionally and socially isolated humans are exactly like emotionally and socially isolated rats, choosing drugs to dull the pain of being alone.

## THE HUMAN RAT PARK

One of the reasons rats are routinely used in psychological experiments is that they are social creatures in many of the same ways that humans are social creatures. Happy rats require stimulation, company, play, drama, sex, and social interaction to stay happy.

Humans add an extra layer to this equation. We also need close attachments to thrive.

The level and caliber of trust and connection experienced in early childhood carries forward into adult life. Those who experience secure attachment as infants, toddlers, and young children carry that into their adult lives, and thus are naturally able to trust and connect in healthy ways. Those who don't experience such secure early life attachment will most often struggle as adults. Securely attached individuals tend to feel comfortable and enjoy the human version of Alexander's rat park, while insecurely attached people typically struggle to fit in and intimately connect.

And we know by now which group is more vulnerable to addiction, right? We also know from Alexander's work that even rats who'd previously been isolated and drinking the drugged water (addicted rats) left it alone when they were placed in his socially stimulating rat park. With a little bit of socialization, their addiction disappeared.

> With proper direction, support, and a fair amount of conscious effort, individuals who were not graced with secure childhood attachments (and therefore the ability to easily and comfortably connect in adulthood) can develop earned security via long-term therapy, faith-based and twelve-step groups, and various other healthy and healing relationships—the most important of which are healthy connections with loved ones.

Happily, this result transfers to humans, though in somewhat more complicated ways. With proper direction, support, and a fair amount of conscious effort, individuals who were not graced with secure childhood attachments (and therefore the ability to easily and comfortably connect in adulthood) can develop earned security via long-term therapy, faith-based and twelve-step groups, and various other healthy and healing relationships—the most important of which are healthy connections with loved ones.

This means the dysfunctional lessons learned by addicts in child-hood can be unlearned (experienced differently) through empathetic and supportive emotional interactions, especially with loving, empa-thetic, healthfully supportive family members and friends. Addicts are not automatically locked for life into a state of isolated self-soothing and self-regulation because they can choose connection.

However, placing human addicts in a room full of people and stimulating activities (as Alexander did with rats) is not quite enough. Human addicts must earn a sense of security and attachment. Rats don't really need to do that because their brains and their psyches are considerably simpler. You can take an addicted rat and toss him into the rat park, and he will quickly and easily assimilate, pushing his addiction to the curb in favor of healthier rat connections and activities.

People? Not so much. With human addicts, there is further work to be done.

## Prescribing Addiction

Before we address the effects of relational trauma as a source of addiction, we must emphatically emphasize that not all addictions come about in the same way. Without question, far too many people become physically addicted to opioids and other prescribed medications that end up hurting them far more than they help. Such medications can lead to otherwise healthy individuals into abuse and addiction. Depending on the length and depth of their addictive struggle, their healing process often involves finding healthier ways to manage physical pain and suffering. But they must also learn the tools of addiction recovery. In the addition world we often hear the phrase once an addict, always an addict. In the case of opioid and other medication-induced addictions, the healing process may begin by weaning people off such drugs to eliminate the physical aspects of their addictive cravings, but for many people this does not end the addictive challenges of those who become psychologically addicted. Those who learn that drugs can—however briefly—profoundly improve their moods while simultaneously blocking out uncomfortable feelings can find themselves struggling with addictive desires and actions that also require incorporating traditional forms of longer-term addiction recovery. Highly profitable, inadequately researched, yet widely distributed medications are routinely sold to doctors in order to meet corporate sales quotas without consideration of the lifelong harm they may cause the user and their families. This defines the process of a prescribed addiction.

## ADDICTION AS A SYMPTOM OF TRAUMA

By the early twenty-first century, the disease model and our understanding of trauma evolved into a cohesive, trauma-based model toward the understanding and treatment of addiction. That stated, there is an equally large (and more difficult to treat) population of long-term chronic addicts whose underlying challenges with addition are formed by early or later life trauma. When we experience meaningful trauma (which differs from person to person), these experiences can disturb our ability to create and lean into deep, meaningful, and intimate, relationships. While healthier people almost always turn to such relationships when feeling stressed, overwhelmed, and dysregulated, addicts will turn to emotional numbing and escape.

Thus, early trauma often affects our ability to attach in healthy ways. The methods that addicts employ to survive these experiences such as dissociation and fantasy often provide the emotional regulation and consistency that their early caregivers did not give. These survival mechanisms are seen as the early foundation for later substance abuse. Such people learn early that it is better to escape painful feelings than it is to rely on intimate family, friends, and community for emotional support. While these unconscious choices for emotional survival may allow them to grow into intellectually functional adults, over time, their lack of faith in others and related avoidance of deep adult intimacies leave them with compulsive and addictive substances and behaviors as their primary source of comfort and self-soothing. To put it simply, by the time such people become adults, they feel safer leaning into addictive substances and behaviors than they do people.

Addicts abuse substances and engage in highly stimulating, dissociative behaviors for different reasons than do healthy people. Since the dawn of time, healthy people have used drugs and alcohol toward greater social engagement, spirituality, pleasure, and relaxation. Addicts, however, abuse the same substances seeking a secondary gain of escape and emotional numbing. Addicts often pretend they are abusing substances and acting out behaviorally to have fun, but in reality they're more focused on losing themselves altogether. Thus, addicts repeatedly return to these same behaviors over and over again expecting different results, which leads to their becoming decreasingly functional adults.

Addicted people live within an endless loop of feeling bad, drinking, using or behaviorally acting out to escape those feelings, and then feel shameful or worse than they did when they started. As they lack the ability to self-soothe and self-regulate, they fall once again into the pit of addiction. And then they repeat the pattern. This is the cycle of addiction.

Today, both the disease model and the role of unresolved early-life trauma in the etiology of addiction are well accepted. As Maté writes, "A hurt is at the center of all addictive behaviors. It is present in the gambler, the internet addict, the compulsive shopper, and the workaholic."[4] This means that addictions form because trauma (neglect, abuse, etc.) has poisoned the well of interpersonal attachment. Thanks to unresolved early-life trauma, addicts learn to associate fear rather than comfort to deep human intimacy and attachment. Thus, they refuse to turn to others, even loved ones, for help when they're struggling or feeling down. Instead, they compulsively and obsessively attempt to self-soothe by numbing out with addictive substances and behaviors.

Unsurprisingly, addiction treatment specialists and the twelve-step community have unconsciously operated with "addictions are an intimacy disorder, and healthy connections are the antidote" as an underlying principle for many decades. In fact, much of what occurs in well-informed, group-focused addiction treatment and twelve-step recovery programs (beyond breaking through the denial and putting a stop to addictive behavior) is geared, either directly or indirectly, toward the development of reliably healthy social bonds. In the therapy field we call this social learning. Admittedly, twelve-step programs are not the right path for every recovering addict. However, those who have found sobriety and peace in places such as AA, NA, SAA, and CMA almost universally find in those environments a safe place to explore, practice, and develop healthy prodependent relationships. And trust me here, addicts don't attend twelve-step meetings for years on end for the coffee and doughnuts. They stick around because the rooms of recovery are where they finally feel like they're part of a healthy, responsive, supportive, and engaged family. And for the most part, they are spot on.

Interestingly, it's not just therapists, support groups, and loved ones who can help addicts. Society at large can also lend a hand. Consider the nation of Portugal. Since decriminalizing illicit drugs in 2001, Portugal has tried very hard to integrate addicts into their communities, offering traditional treatment and counseling plus subsidized jobs and quite a lot of social programming. Basically, Portugal has made a nationwide effort to help addicts connect with the world and the people around them. And it's working, too. Problematic drug use is down, including adolescent drug use, drug-related harms, and drug-related deaths.[5] Portugal's strategy of connecting and rewarding instead of incarcerating (exiling, isolating, and disconnecting) addicts has been highly effective.

And why would we expect anything different? After all, as we have discussed, it's an essential part of the human condition to attach emotionally and to lean into our attachments. Our need for connection is as fundamental to life, health, and happiness as our needs for food, water, and shelter. When our needs for intimacy and attachment go unmet, we struggle. End of story.

That said, developing healthy intimate connections can be difficult, especially for addicts, who, as discussed, nearly always have histories of chronic childhood trauma and other forms of early life dysfunction that make intimate attachment uncomfortable and difficult. For addicts, learning to trust, reducing shame, and feeling comfortable with emotional and social vulnerability takes time, ongoing effort, and a knowledgeable, willing, and empathetic support network (therapists, fellow recovering addicts, friends, employers, and loved ones). The good news is that both research and countless thousands of healthy, happy, long-sober addicts have shown us that such healing can turn an isolated and addicted life into one of peace and connection.

## ADDICTION TREATMENT

When working with addicts, therapists use a wide variety of treatment methodologies; some are behavior based, some are trauma based while others are more focused on attachment, etc. Whatever modality is used, addicts nearly always need, first and foremost, a giant dose of reality. Beyond initial sobriety and ensuring they are stable enough to begin treatment, breaking through the façade of denial that allows them to use with (internal) impunity is task one. Little forward movement can occur until they understand and view their addiction as the destructive force that it is.

Once denial cracks, which can be a difficult and time-consuming process, a plan for ongoing sobriety (that incorporates lots and lots of truth-telling, trust-building, and accountability) can be implemented. Usually, this plan incorporates a mix of individual therapy, addiction-focused group therapy, cognitive behavioral work, social learning, and twelve-step or similar support groups. Ultimately, addiction treatment recognizes that the disease of addiction is, more than anything else, an intimacy disorder, and these various approaches tend to work mostly because they encourage healthy human interactions and connection.

At some point, addicts are also asked to identify and eventually address the underlying emotional deficits and trauma that led them into addiction in the first place. At minimum, reviewing a client's trauma history helps to reduce shame. Essentially, this effort tells addicts, "You're not an addict because you're a bad person. You're an addict because you are a broken person, because some bad things happened when you were younger, and you cleverly learned to escape your painful emotions by numbing out. Unfortunately, you're still handling your problems by escaping from them instead of turning to others for help in dealing with them. But that is something that we can fix."

Whichever approaches are utilized in treatment, the work required for early addiction healing looks something like this:

- Uncover and explore denial and misguided thinking.
- Stop the drinking/using/acting out.
- Identify the addictive patterns.
- Engage in immediate crisis management re family, work, parenting, finances, etc.
- Identify addiction triggers (the people, places, and things that precipitate a need/desire to use).
- Identify and implement alternatives to using (relapse prevention).
- Note and explore past trauma in order to reduce shame by validating the reason this person has become an addict.
- Develop earned security through prodependent connections with clinicians, fellow recovering addicts, friends, and most importantly, loved ones.
- Repeat.

So, once again, treating addicts ultimately focuses on the development of prodependent connections with loved ones and other important individuals. Simply stated, effective addiction treatment encourages and facilitates a transition away from unwanted dependencies on drugs and/or compulsive behaviors toward inter-personal dependency. Recovering addicts have learned the impor-tance of leaning into the support of reliable others, and for those with long-term sobriety, this slowly becomes their new normal. When loved ones of addicts are healthfully prodependent, it's easier for addicts to feel safely connected. And when addicts feel safely con-nected, it's easier to stay sober.

# Chapter Seven

# PRODEPENDENCE IN ACTION

*If a problem can't be solved within the frame it was conceived, the
solution lies in reframing the problem.*[1]

—Brian McGreevy, *Hemlock Grove*

## A LOVED ONE'S ROLE IN THE HEALING PROCESS

As stated earlier, addicts learn, early in life, from thousands
of small interactions plus a couple of highly formative ones,
that relying on others for emotional support is hurtful and
chaotic and best avoided. Our normal, human desire to be intimate and close to others powerfully conflicts with their deep, early
fears that such closeness will bring more pain and emptiness. This
evokes feelings of isolation and sadness, which are readily escaped
via addiction. They choose to or are not able to be open and to be
vulnerable with people, actions that are required to build meaningful

attachments in adult life. As such, addicts are unlikely to reach out for help no matter how badly they need it. This is reflective of their formative early experiences, which left them feeling untrusting, unworthy, and ashamed. When facing stress, conflict, and the like, despite their outward bravado, addicts tend to turn inward by beating themselves up with shame and self-hatred rather than reaching outward for supportive others.

This is where caregiving loved ones come in. As discussed earlier, one of the most effective ways to overcome addiction is for addicts to develop healthy, meaningful, ongoing interpersonal connections. Unquestionably, the most important of those connections are with their family and loved ones who can become an integral and ongoing part of an addict's recovery, encouraging them to slowly and steadily develop a secure emotional foundation, develop earned security, and help an addict heal from addiction long-term.

---

### Twelve-Step Groups for Loved Ones of Addicts

I fully endorse, encourage, and deeply believe in the meaningful support that programs such as Al-Anon and ACoA offer to those fortunate enough to attend them. Having been a lifelong participant in such environments, I'm forever grateful to the experience and the people in those rooms. To witness what occurs in recovery meetings is to witness prodependent healing in action. The peer support, shame reduction, and social bonding offered within such groups, combined with the shared language and perspective they create, can be immeasurably useful toward helping loved ones move past the fear and hopelessness wrought by active addiction. Such groups—day in and day out and absolutely free—provide both a structured process and a loving community to all those working toward the common goal of healing their family and their life.

Today, I am more thoughtful when encouraging caregiving loved ones to attend and participate in these groups. The faster we can get an addict into twelve-step recovery, the better. However, trusted, loving family members may not be ready for this type of support because they can interpret such suggestions as a sign that: (a) there is something wrong with them, or (b) they have been maintaining someone else's addiction. Prodependence advises that it is preferable to educate loved ones about the nature of the addictive process along with the differences between codependency and prodependence before encouraging them to attend such support groups. The goal here is to avoid their taking the message that somehow they are at fault for the addict's problems. From a prodependent lens, we don't suggest that loved ones attend twelve-step recovery groups until they have fully grasped and integrated the fact that *they are in no way* for another person's addiction or relapse.

Making active use of trusted relationships allows addicts to find sobriety and remain sober. The support, consistency and role-modeling proffered by such intimacies also helps to ease the pain of uncovering and processing the trauma of addiction. While some addicts will chose to do this work solely through therapy, others will find their way by committing long-term to supportive groups such as AA, NA, SAA, GA and the like. Those who are fortunate enough to have the financial resources may do both. Regardless of the path taken, finding and maintaining sobriety can be incredibly difficult, time consuming and for some—very expensive. Yet that journey is one worth taking because over time it has led many addicts from shame to grace.

# SAFETY FIRST!

As discussed throughout this book, prodependence unquestion-ably encourages and supports remaining actively involved with an addicted loved one as they struggle to heal. And yet there are cir-cumstances where it is clearly unsafe to self and others to be around the addict 24/7, live with them or even have contact with them at all.

Deep insight into various forms of abuse and the road out of them are beyond the scope of this text. Abuse survivors need hands on help from trusted friends, clergy, therapists and others. Some need to change the locks, some need to leave for their own safety while others need therapeutic tools such as taking a time out or texting their anger rather than doing so live. There is a lot of local and national help out there for those experiencing abuse—from legal support to clinical guidance and back. Nearly all that information can be found online. Sadly many survivors will feel too embarrassed or ashamed to seek outside help, while others may feel that they are not deserving of the help they need. Without question, those being harmed in their own homes and elsewhere (especially via physical and sexual abuse) need outside help. Sadly the hardest part may be getting them to seek it.

One of the most painful experiences in the addiction dynamic happens when addicts abuse beloved spouses, parents, children, and close others. Violence, blaming, yelling, gaslighting, sexual abuse and intimidation are among the many forms this can take. Beyond the abuse itself, it's emotionally overwhelming to have someone you trust and love hurt you over and over again. Who wants to believe that someone who has professed to care about you can turn on a dime and be abusive? Thus it's typical for overwhelmed caring, intimate family loved ones to say things like, "If you say you love me, how can you do and say things like that?" These statements are readily understandable given the circumstances. But the answer to this question is fairly simple as most addicts compartmentalize their lives in ways that allow them to love someone and do things to hurt them at the same time.

It's a sad truth that many addicts will hurt those they love when high and sometimes when sober. Addicts with a history of abusing people in the past are of the most concern as this abuse will often escalate in sync with the addiction itself.

## WHEN LOVE HURTS

In a relationship where there is addiction or other chronic mental illness, the abuse experienced can be less obvious than physical violence. In just a few examples among many, this happens in situations where an addict makes financial decisions without a loved one's knowledge or gets arrested without telling anyone, or picks up the kids at school when high. Other forms of non-violent abuse include name-calling, devaluing, blaming, or turning family and friends against them. Many addicts will act out sexually with or without their spouse's knowledge, an act that often produces its own type of betrayal trauma.

Unsurprisingly it's not just addicts who can act out in this way. Loved ones can also express rage, hurt, and disappointment by being abusive. The pressure of neglected children, finances and commitments can lead to non-addicts yelling, breaking things, or being physically abusive. After acting this way they may comment, "I don't know how I can do this. It's like I've become someone I never wanted to be. How did I get here?"

It's not unusual in such circumstances for there to be abuse on both sides. These actions tend to be more impulsive and situational than malicious, most often driven by rage, grief, hurt, abandonment, and other deeper emotions. That said, regardless of why, how or who it happens, acting out abusively is counterproductive, destructive and at times outright dangerous.

How does abuse affect people over time? Many report extreme fear, hypervigilance, obsession, numbness, and a variety of emotional and physical symptoms when interacting with the struggling individual. They feel like they are walking on eggshells just waiting for the next verbal or emotional attack or betrayal to occur. Insecurity abounds as the relationship is consistently unreliable inconsistent and constantly in flux. Struggling addicts will manipulate by using mind games like gaslighting that can leave loved ones doubting their own sense of reality.

Prodependence does not espouse the idea that loved ones should stay in an intimate relationship with the addict simply because they naturally desire to remain attached and bonded; rather it acknowledges the healthy desire for them to retain these connections even when they are no longer a safe and viable option. Prodependence teaches how to push the addictive relationship aside for survival and stability, when necessary, fully knowing those actions may or may not influence change in the addict. But change happens even in the most unlikely of circumstances. Beyond immediate safety issues that may require separation, prodependence suggests that larger permanent decisions about staying or leaving the relationship be delayed until the crisis has passed while all involved have achieved greater emotional and physical stability.

Safety is the key. Without safety and trust there is no sustainable connection or effective attachment for anyone. No safety, no growth.

# ABUSE AND THE PRODEPENDENCE MODEL

The prodependence model addresses abuse by seeking to understand and confront the negative and harmful behavior using whatever tools necessary toward establishing personal and familial safety. Unlike the codependency model that would encourage the loved one to focus primarily on their part in the problem and completely detach from the addict for safety, prodependence sees the abusive behavior for what it is: abusive behavior.

Prodependence does not require that anyone take responsibility for another's abuse, although the tendency of most abusive people is to externalize the source of their anger. Rather, the model asks us to work toward identification and elimination from the very start, rather than any focus on insight. Abuse in any form, by anyone involved, must be the primary focus until all parties are guaranteed physical and emotional safety, regardless of how this is achieved.

In summary, prodependence:
- Acknowledges the reality and effects of abuse within the relationship.
- Focuses on the source of a loved one's distress.
- Celebrates a desire for safe and meaningful connection.
- Recognizes the distress of loved ones as a trauma response.
- Encourages safe attachment when/where/if possible.
- Encourages personal and interpersonal safety (physical, verbal, etc.) over remaining with the addict (abuser).

# PRODEPENDENCE DOES NOT MEAN LIVING WITH ABUSE

Prodependence holds no tolerance for abuse, even though the model does not encourage detachment. However, without question, prodependence, as does any ethical and effective treatment model, strongly encourages self-preservation on every level. People should be helped to create an appropriate and useful safety plan. Prodependence is fully focused on helping troubled people find deeper connection, meaning, and healing through their relationships, but never at the cost of one's health, safety, well-being, or sanity. Sometimes, the most loving and supportive thing to do is to withdraw, especially when personal safety is of primary concern.

## MOVE ON OR STAY?

A dilemma with which betrayed loved ones frequently wrestle is when they should stay and when they should leave a relationship. First and foremost, the decision to remain in or exit a relationship is a personal choice. There is no scenario in which any of us can make that choice for a another, either as a helping professional or a friend or loved one of those in a challenging situation. All professionals have an ethical responsibility to help keep our clients safe. This can be challenging as each client's specific needs for safety may differ. There are situations that may obviously require physical distance for safety and then there are those that may not be so apparent. Just like each vessel on the water has a unique Plimsoll line that determines how much load weight it can handle before taking on water and sinking; so do loved one have their own "internal Plimsoll line" that determines their individual limit for what they can manage in a given relationship. Assisting the others to navigate their own boundaries and limits is very useful, even if that means encouraging a loving person the relationship for their own well-being.

Remaining emotionally and physically close to an addict who is using or newly sober requires that the addict is:

- Not being abusive—physical, verbal, sexual.
- Actively seeking help and intervention for himself or herself.
- Is aware that his or her addictive problems are his or her to fix and not the fault of parents, partners, and the like.
- Is taking responsibility for his or her actions and decisions.
- Has moments of empathy and compassion for people and situations in which he or she has caused harm.
- Initiating and maintaining his or her own recovery-self-care (twelve-step meetings, therapies, etc.) without having to be nagged, begged, or pushed into doing the right thing.

Examples of situations in which loved one may choose (or need) to leave include:

- The addict is actively abusive, even dangerous physically, emotionally, financially, etc., and is clearly causing harm.
- No longer willing to help or support the addict.
- No longer wanting to remain in the relationship.
- A lack of safety.
- Frustrated loved ones are themselves persistently being abusive.
- The addict remains in denial and unwilling to consider addressing the addiction.
- The addict continues cycles of abuse with partner and/or other loved ones.
- The addict refuses to be honest and transparent.
- The addict's behavior leaves family, loved ones, or spouse in an endless cycle of blame and chaos.

- Living in repeating cycles of anger, frustration, and disappointment.

## PRODEPENDENT SUPPORT AND THERAPY

Prodependence is an interpersonal attachment and strength-based model that sees a caregiving loved one's commitment to helping an addicted family member as both heroic and reasonable given the gravity of the injuries (and other crises) they've experienced in the relationship.

Prodependence is based on the following tenets:

- Human beings are internally wired for secure attachment and pair-bonding (interdependence).
- Disruptions in such attachments can create a primal pain response.
- A primal pain response initiates a sense of crisis.
- An active crisis state stops the individual from accessing his or her intellectual self.
- Individuals in this state will often engage in frantic (and sometimes misguided) attempts to stop and/or control the crisis that is the source of their emotional instability.
- An addict's choice to abuse substances or act out behaviorally should never be ascribed to the faults of the family, partner, or caretaker. Addicts use because they choose to use. Period.
- It is abusive to put responsibility on anyone other than the addict for the addict's decision to use or behaviorally act out.
- Loved ones of addicts are deeply affected by the addict's instability on an almost daily basis.

- Loved ones of addicts experience painful losses and circumstances due to the addiction.
- The desire to help or save an addicted loved one should never be viewed as pathological.
- No pathology should ever be ascribed to someone's attempts in trying to rescue, save, or control a loved one who is out of control.
- No one can be addicted to another person.
- It is not possible to "love too much."
- Trying to save a troubled loved one is hero's work that should be validated and normalized.
- No caregiver can offer perfectly aligned support. Some of what caregivers do may work and some may not, but it is unacceptable to blame them for not having given in "the right way" or the most productive way.
- Crisis intervention techniques and modalities are best utilized in such situations to help loved ones regain as much emotional and intellectual equilibrium as possible, often while in the midst of navigating painful, unstable circumstances.
- The therapist's goal is to stabilize, normalize, and help such clients find their way forward. Nothing more, nothing less.

With prodependence, caregiving loved ones of addicts are not automatically viewed as having an illness requiring treatment. Instead of viewing caregivers as part of the disease, prodependence views them as being in crisis and behaving as anyone in crisis would naturally

> Instead of viewing caregivers as part of the disease, prodependence views them as being in crisis and behaving as anyone in crisis would naturally behave.

behave. Caregivers are not thought of as struggling because of an inherent pathology (or even a pseudo-pathology), rather, they are thought of as struggling because they:

- Are deeply involved with someone who is falling apart right in front of their eyes despite their attempts to assist and save that person.
- Find themselves inadvertently behaving in ways that cause them to feel badly about themselves, like nagging, yelling, threatening, hitting, raging, judging, etc.
- Are confused, exhausted, and overwhelmed (thus in crisis) because they've been doing their job and the addict's job within the family, often for years on end.
- Feel defeated, unloved, unappreciated, and hopeless due to the addict's inability to stop using (despite their best efforts to help).
- Are often being verbally psychologically manipulated.
- Are being emotionally violated via affairs, sexual acting out, and the like.

When offering prodependent treatment for loved ones of addicts, a supportive professional should do the following:

- Assess for any and all physical and emotional violations.
- Assess for any genuine pathology (depression, anxiety, PTSD, mood disorders, and the like).
- Validate and celebrate prior attempts to rescue, save, heal, and otherwise help the addict.
- Educate about the nature of addiction and the stress it can place on loved ones.
- Identify times and situations where a loved one's actions have led to a less than ideal outcome, and redirect toward more effective assistance.

- Provide ongoing support.
- Work to establish, implement, and maintain healthy boundaries.
- Work to improve the client's efforts at self-care—exercise, recreation, spirituality, creativity, etc.
- Learn what to do when the addict is high or upset.

## CODEPENDENCY OR CRISIS?

Realizing that someone you love is an addict is difficult and confusing. Always. It's not just the pain of specific bad behaviors, it's the loss of trust. This leaves caregiving loved ones in a daze—stunned, hurt, uncertain, and unable to fully assimilate and accept what is happening. Loss of trust in someone you love leaves family, friends, and spouses saying thing such as, "How can I believe anything you say or do?" Or, "How do we know what you are doing or where you are going whenever you leave the house?" And to repeat, ongoing unresolved addition pushes loved ones into crisis.

At its core, prodependence states that the most useful and effective early form of support for those emotionally involved with an active addict is crisis intervention treatment. If we agree that being emotionally attached to an active addict can push those close to them into a crisis, then we already have a successful treatment model in place to meet their needs. By leading with a method that more fully aligns with where the client is today, we avoid codependency theory while supporting them in real time. To move in this direction, we need to more clearly elucidate a definition for the word *crisis*:

Crisis is a state of emotional turmoil or an acute emotional reaction to a powerful stimulus or demand.

There are three characteristics of crisis:

1) The usual balance between thinking and emotions has become disturbed.

2) The ways someone typically copes with day-to-day stress, such as exercise, time with friends, hobbies, work satisfaction, and the like, are overwhelmed by the crisis and no longer provide enough distraction and enjoyment to help the person feel stable.

3) Evidence of impairment in an individual or family.

Crisis intervention methods are meant to provide help to individuals or groups during a period of extreme distress. This kind of therapy is, by design, temporary, active and supportive.

Supporting others toward moving out of crisis mode abides by the following seven principals: [2]

1) Simplicity: In a crisis, people respond best to simple procedures. Simple things have the best chance of having a positive effect.

2) Brevity: Emotional and psychological first aid needs to remain short, from a few minutes up to one hour.

3) Concrete Direction and Support: Based on the person's needs for help.

4) Pragmatism and Validation: Keep it practical. Impractical suggestions can cause the person to feel more frustrated and out of control. Encourage healthy functioning.

5) Working in the Here and Now: People in a crisis don't have the psychological sophistication to engage in in-depth evaluations or discussions of the past. Remain focused on the problems at hand.

6) Offer Hope: Set up expectations of a reasonable positive outcome. Encourage the person in crisis to recognize that help is present, there is hope and the situation is manageable.

7) Normalize their experience.

Note that several of the above suggestions are antithetical to the codependence model. Working in the here and now, offering concrete direction and support, having therapy and other support, be brief, targeted, and simple are not methods that codependent treatment would support. Prodependence says that helping people in these circumstance means remaining focused on how they can get through today, tomorrow, and maybe next week, not issues from their past. The focus for prodependent support is on working through current problems period.

In simple terms, this person needs:

- Validation of their intuition and feelings.
- Acknowledgment and appreciation for the love and care they provide.
- Simple direction and structure to help them get by day to day.
- Education about addiction and the family dynamics of recovery.
- Insight into the effects that lies, manipulation, and secrets have on loved ones of addicts.
- Concrete direction regarding in-the-moment and longer-term self-care.
- Useful advice on setting and maintaining healthy boundaries with the addict and others.
- Hope.
- Repeat.

You will know if you are working with a prodependent therapist or guide as such professionals are trained to avoid questions and direction that might lead to a loved one feeling responsible for the addict's behavior. Prodependent support means that the helper avoids the following:

- Implying that another's attempts to help are a sign of pathology in the helper.
- Suggesting that deep love and a desire to help a loved one are anything but normal and healthy.
- Leaving someone with the idea or suggestion that they are somehow contributing to the addict's choice to use or act out.
- Asking them to look at "their part."
- Exploring a loved one's early childhood and family history.
- Asking clients to learn more about their "codependent" behaviors.
- Diagnosing this person (as codependent, bipolar, borderline, or anything else) to explain their distress.
- Implying that their own unresolved past trauma is driving their current reactivity.
- Underestimating the client's understandable fears and insecurity by implying that they are overreacting or responding to their own unconscious issues.
- Assuming the client must be codependent or otherwise troubled, thereby disregarding their current circumstances and needs.
- Sending a client too soon to twelve-step or other support groups that will put some of the responsibility for another's addiction on them.

In the early stages of the crisis stage of treatment, the actions described above are not helpful because it can lead caregivers to conclude (as per codependency) that they are part of the problem. After all, why would a supportive counselor or clergy be so focused on them and their past if they are not partially at fault?

Additional training and guidance for addiction counselors, therapists, and clergy practicing in this arena can be found in *Practicing Prodependence: The Clinical Alternative to Codependency Treatment.*

## FEELINGS ARE NOT FACTS

Loved ones of addicts also need therapists and others to understand, accept, and validate that they have every right to feel angry, hurt, confused, and mistrustful. Thus, they may understandably rage, split, decompensate, do detective work, enmesh, enable, control, try to get opinions from anyone they can find, and more. This represents their understandable reactivity and desire to help however they can.

Instead of being confrontational or overtly directive with such people, we encourage those supporting them to be invitational. We are more helpful by focusing them to healthfully and effectively support the addict with useful boundaries and self-care. Prodependence discourages preaching distance from the problem as so many codependency therapists, self-help books, and groups currently do. Instead, we teach the healthy structure required to more effectively help themselves and the addict all the while celebrating their need to maintain stable intimate connections. And this is the foundation of prodependent therapy.

## LOVED ONES CAN BE THE LAST (YET MOST IMPORTANT) CONNECTION

For reasons already discussed, intimate connections are difficult for addicts, including addicts who are early in the recovery process.

Because of this, addicts new to sobriety often find it easier to connect and be supported through external sources such as therapy, church groups, twelve-step recovery, and other addiction-focused support networks. These "less important" connections are less threatening to newly recovering addicts. This can be confusing and traumatic for family members, who feel shunned when the addict opts to connect with and rely on others but not them.

## WHAT ABOUT ME?

A caregiving loved one's job during this trying period is to be there in healthy, prodependent ways when the addict is ready and willing to accept the loved one's support, even if that means the loved one is the last person invited to the recovery party. Caregivers need to understand that when the addict pushes them away, it's not because the addict doesn't love and care about them, and it's not because the addict doesn't want to be cared for and loved by them; it's because the addict feels unworthy of love and support, especially from the people who "know them" the best. This is why we can drop a human addict into a healthy social situation—the human version of the rat park— and they are unlikely to recover without further effort. People with attachment wounds don't overcome those problems simply by being around other people. They need to safely connect on an emotionally intimate level. They need to develop earned security. And for addicts that is easier accomplished, at least initially, with relative strangers rather than family members.

That said, it's pretty awful for caregiving loved ones when an addict is willing to become emotionally connected with and to accept support from a therapist, a priest, a sponsor, friends, and fellow recovering addicts and not them. But starting with those far away and slowly working back to intimately attach with those who are closer and more important is often an addict's pathway to connection.

## TRUST IS BUILT FROM THE OUTSIDE IN

Addicts must take baby steps in recovery, learning to become vulnerable (and to accept the rewards of doing this) one small step at a time. This can leave others feeling angry or concerned when the addict starts being more open and vulnerable with outsiders (say those in twelve-step recovery or therapy groups), then they are with them. And this makes a lot of sense from their perspective, i.e., "When you were using or acting out you kept so much from me but now strangers hear more about you than I do!" While it may seem counterintuitive, at the start of recovery the less important and intimate a relationship is to the addict, the easier time they have taking emotional risks. When viewed in this way, the last people with whom the addict would want to be vulnerable (and truly intimate) are the relationships where they have the most to lose. It is essential that therapists and loved ones gain this insight into the healing process.

That said, it is never acceptable for the addict who is already in a committed, intimate relationship to use "addiction healing" as an opportunity to disappear into behavioral addictions like eating, gambling, or sex. Acting badly in ways that lead to more deception and shame is the fastest road to relapse.

## WHERE DO LOVED ONES TURN FOR SUPPORT?

In the midst of crisis, the natural thing for a person to do is to turn to a loved one for support. That person loves you, and you love them, so you are going to be there to support one another. And the closer you are to that person, the more likely it is that they will be able and willing to care for you. Unless, of course, that loved one is an addict. Because addicts just don't connect in this way.

My colleague Michelle Mays refers to this conundrum—the desire to turn to a loved one for support even though that person, because of an addiction, is ill-equipped to respond in healthy, empathetic, supportive ways—as the no man's land of recovery.[3] Usually, loved ones of addicts are all too familiar with this space. They innately know that they need to connect with a loved one to heal the attachment deficit they feel, but their loved one, because they are addicted, can't provide the needed support and connection.

Let's face it, it can be embarrassing for anyone to turn to clergy, doctors, neighbors, or parents for help with addiction. Here again, we bump up against the near universal stigma working against both addicts and those who care for them.

## FINDING SUPPORT OUTSIDE THE RELATIONSHIP

Even when the addict is doing everything possible to establish and maintain sobriety, the pain that they have caused to caregiving loved ones is often too deep and too fresh for the addict to be trusted and relied upon in any meaningful emotional way. As such, the addict is poorly suited to providing support even if they were psychologically willing to do so, which, for reasons already discussed, is unlikely in early recovery. This realization can be painful for both parties. They know that they love and care for one another, but the addiction has driven a wedge between them that makes healthy intimacy difficult.

In time, this will change. In the early stages of healing, however, loved ones of addicts, like addicts themselves, typically need to look elsewhere for support—to  prodependence-oriented therapists, to friends who can empathize with and validate their experience, and to support groups that can help them focus, at least a little bit, on caring for themselves as well as their addicted loved one. And yes, this type of support can be found in groups such as ACoA and Al-Anon— as long as the individual focuses on the work at hand (boundaries, self-care, attending to themselves as well as their troubled loved one) while not buying into the belief that their love, support, and caregiving is unhealthy.

## SELF-CARE

As stated above, when working with loved ones of addicts, there are three primary areas of focus: self-soothing when overwhelmed, self-care, and healthy boundaries. Often, convincing loved ones to concentrate, even a little bit, on their own well-being is the hardest and most difficult task.

When dealing with caregiving loved ones who are reluctant to also care for themselves, I sometimes remind them that on airplanes, flight attendants instruct passengers on safety procedures in the event of an emergency. One of their primary instructions is that, if oxygen masks are needed, parents should affix their mask first, and then affix masks on their children. This directive recognizes a fundamental tenet of life: If you're not taking adequate care of yourself, you're likely to be a poor caregiver for others. This is especially true when dealing with an addict—especially as they too tend to suck all the air out of the room.

Nevertheless, self-care often sounds selfish to caregiving loved ones, even though it's not. Unless, of course, the person flips to the opposite extreme and completely stops caring for others. Detaching to that degree is as unhealthy as focusing on others to the point where one forgets to care for oneself. Self-care does not mean caring for oneself instead of the addict, it means caring for oneself as well as the addict.

> With prodependence, self-care is about finding a middle ground that is healthy for the caregiver, for the addict, and for the relationship between the caregiver and the addict.

With prodependence, self-care is about finding a middle ground that is healthy for the caregiver, for the addict, and for the relationship between the caregiver and the addict. Living in the extremes—doing too much too often or detaching completely and forcing the addict to struggle without assistance—is not healthy for anyone. Living in one or the other of these extremes perpetuates the addiction, along with insecure attachment, family dysfunction, and an unhappy life.

Still, engaging in self-care may feel counterintuitive to caregiving loved ones who are so used to focusing on someone else. Many learned in childhood to disregard their own needs in order to focus on the wants and desires of others. In such cases, taking time to care for oneself (without detachment) may nonetheless feel selfish or decadent. For individuals who are used to being ignored, deprived, used or shamed, as loved ones of addicts often are, pausing to engage in even a small amount of self-care and self-nurturance typically requires external guidance, support, conscious planning, and the support of others.

## Codependence à la Carte Is Still Codependence

While writing this book, I spoke to many professionals and laypeople about the current use of the term and model of codependency. My thanks to you for offering your time, beliefs, experiences, interpretations, and opinions. What I have heard nearly universally is that we have a shared need for a new, fully articulated, differently focused model for the treatment of addict's loved ones— one that goes beyond the blame and interpersonal limitations of codependency.

It appears to me, after these conversations, that many therapy, clergy and addiction therapists are already on this new path, even though they have lacked terminology or a guidebook to light the way. In our discussions many such professionals have said things to me such as:

- I use an adapted version of the codependency model, but mine is more attachment focused.
- I see codependence as a developmental issue, as laid out in some of the later writings on the subject, and not as much about early-life trauma, as many others tend to view it.
- I use the word *codependent,* but I don't use that actual model for treatment because my clients typically don't respond well to it.
- I work from adaptive, later versions of the codependence model, ones written long after the original model was proposed. And even then, I focus more on healthy attachment than detachment.
- I don't do much, if any, trauma exploration at the start when I'm treating loved ones of addicts. I use more of a crisis-driven model.

To you I say, "Great job! You have already found (or are finding) your way to prodependent, attachment-focused treatment for caregiving loved ones of addicts and other troubled individuals, and you were doing this before I ever put pen to paper. I celebrate your useful additions and adaptations to this new model of prodependence. Moreover, your thoughtful input has helped me evolve the theories that are the foundation of this book."

That said, I cannot rely on or recommend that professionals or laypeople utilize an adapted or updated version of the codependence model as many choose to do. As stated, there is no formal standard for this model, but there are 400-plus books on the topic—all written without a criteria-based description of the problem. Regardless of which version of codependency is adopted it will always be a model that asks loved ones to examine the ways that their own past is affecting their current circumstances.

## BOUNDARIES

Many addicts try to get healthy and succeed. They get sober, they stay sober, and they slowly overcome the trauma and other issues that have kept them "apart from" instead of "a part of." Other addicts repeatedly try and fail to get sober. Sometimes they have no real interest in sobriety, even if they pretend otherwise. And these outcomes have very little, if anything at all, to do with the loved ones who care for them. An addict's sobriety is not dependent on their loved ones. Recovery is the purview of the addict and no one else.

Still, loved ones of addicts feel responsible for the safety, well-being, and recovery of the addict. Because of this, they often find themselves doing one or more of the following:

- Taking care of things that are the addict's responsibility, not theirs.
- Doing things they don't want to do because they feel like they have no choice.

- Meeting (what they perceive to be) the addict's needs without the addict asking for help.
- Forcing their assistance on the addict, even when that assistance is not wanted or needed.
- Giving without receiving.
- Focusing more on the emotional and relational drama of the addict than on their own problems.
- Making excuses for and/or covering up the problematic behavior of the addict.
- Becoming indispensable to the addict as a way of keeping the addict close.
- Trying to control the addict's behavior as a way of keeping the addict safe.
- Drinking or using with them to keep an eye on them.

Consider the words of Hayley, the thirty-two-year-old wife of an alcoholic:

I was sure that if I could just do a better job with the house and kids, cook better meals, be better in bed, and convince him of my love for him, he would stop drinking. I honestly thought that if I could just be the perfect wife, he would sober up and everything would be okay, and we would finally be happy. What I didn't understand was that drinking was his problem to fix, not mine.

If you can think of it, I probably tried it. But nothing I did worked. He just kept on drinking, and his life—our life—continued to fall apart. I found myself trying to manage and control one crisis after another while micromanaging every aspect of his life. I continued to do this even when I knew it was making me miserable. I just couldn't stop. I was too afraid of the consequences. I worried that if I didn't stop him from drinking, he might get another drunk driving ticket and go to jail for many months, or he might drink and drive and kill someone and go to jail for many years, or he might drink and drive and kill himself. Then there was the fear that if I pushed him too hard to get sober, he would get angry and leave me. Still, I couldn't stop yelling and screaming and manipulating and fixing and doing all sorts of other things to control the addiction. Eventually, I was so busy trying to manage his life that I wasn't living my own.

## BOUNDARIES MATTER

Hayley's desire to bond with and care for her husband, coupled with her anxiety about being alone and unloved, caused her to try to control aspects of her husband's life that were not hers to control. She meant well, but she tried to do too much. Her lack of boundaries and attempts to manage her husband and his alcoholism were a far cry from the healthy, prodependent interaction that he (and she) needed. In time, her "protection" became a prison in which she and her husband were confined.

Hayley, rather obviously, needed help with healthier boundaries. However, like many loved ones of addicts, she didn't understand that many of her efforts to care for her husband were, in fact, counterproductive. She did not understand that by nagging, enabling, and trying to control, she took away her husband's sense of responsibility, along with his ability to make decisions and solve problems, learn from his mistakes, grow as a person, and achieve sobriety, recovery, and healing.

In therapy, rather than point this out to Hayley (as per codependence), I complimented her on her fortitude and for sticking with her husband even in the face of addiction. Then we talked about how tiring and emotionally draining this was for her. Eventually, I suggested that there might be some better, more effective, and less draining ways for her to care for her husband, letting her know that would likely involve setting some boundaries.

To this, Hayley responded as many loved ones of addicts do, saying, "I've done that. I've set boundaries, and he's broken them. Over and over. It doesn't work. He won't change his behavior just because I set a boundary."

I smiled at Hayley's response. Loved ones of addicts often seem to think that setting boundaries is about putting limits on the addict's behavior. And inevitably they've learned, as does anyone who has tried to control the behavior of another person (who's over the age of twelve), that this does not work—at all. Because other people don't want to be controlled by us any more than we want to be controlled by them.

This means that caregivers must focus on their own safety and not depend on the addict to agree with or follow relationship boundaries. I explained this boundary basic to Hayley using my two favorite analogies for boundaries. The first analogy is that healthy boundaries are about staying in our own hula hoop, meaning the only things we can control or that we should try to control are the items within our immediate space—the things that fit within our hula hoop. The second analogy is that we must sometimes look at a situation that's out of control and say, "Not my circus, not my monkeys." If a problem is not of our making, then it's probably not ours to control or fix, and we should leave it alone.

I also explained to Hayley that the purpose of healthy boundaries is to facilitate healthy relationships, not to shut relationships down.

> Healthy boundaries are not about keeping other people out; they're about letting other people safely in.

Healthy boundaries are not about keeping other people out; they're about letting other people safely in. If other people are behaving in ways that are safe for us, we can choose to let them in. If they are behaving in ways that are not safe for us, we can choose to keep them out.

Their behavior belongs to them; our choice belongs to us.

## HELPING THE HELPER

Finally, I let Hayley know that when properly implemented, healthy boundaries prevent enabling, enmeshment, and unwarranted attempts at control. In this way, boundaries protect caregivers from the addict's bad behavior, and, just as importantly, they protect the addict from the caregiver's bad behavior. In time, with healthy boundaries, a caregiver and an addict can establish and maintain healthy interdependence in their relationship.

That said, boundaries are not a one-size-fits-all proposition. Boundaries that are helpful in some relationships could be very unhelpful in others. Recognizing this, I generally ask loved ones of addicts, such as Hayley, to answer the following questions before attempting to define and implement healthy boundaries:

- How deeply mired in addiction is your loved one? Does the addiction completely control their life and thought process, or can they (at least occasionally) make intelligent, rational, well-reasoned decisions?
- Would pulling back and letting the addict face the consequences

of the addiction be helpful in terms of motivating their recovery?

- What would those consequences likely be? Are those consequences something that you and the rest of the family can live with?
- What aspect of the addiction frightens you most? What aspect of the addiction do you most want (and try) to control? Is this a fear that you can rationally and legitimately release?
- Is this a situation where the best thing would be to do more and not less? Despite everyone's desire to see the addict assume responsibility for themselves, could this be a situation where more of you (as a caregiver) is needed?
- Could it be time to hold steady on the reins and not let go?

Healthy boundaries need to be set on a case-by-case basis. What works for one relationship might not work for another. Moreover, the creation of healthy boundaries can mean pulling back on control, as with Hailey and her husband, or taking more control, as we will see in the example that closes this chapter. And sometimes the difference between the two situations is not entirely clear. That is the difficulty faced by loved ones of addicts. As such, the process of finding what works and what doesn't is a matter of trial and error. Moreover, what works and what doesn't work may change over time as the addict starts to heal and become more accountable. As a prodependence-oriented therapist, my job is to facilitate the process of setting and maintaining healthy boundaries (in either direction) while encouraging motivation, structured change, and hope.

No matter how frustrated anyone may at times get with a loved one's seeming inability to implement healthy boundaries, we need to remember that telling them to "just stop enabling and controlling" is about as useful as telling an addict to "just stop using." So, not at all. A better, more prodependent approach is to help the caregiver build healthy interdependence and connection with the addict over time by establishing boundaries that are realistic and workable for that person in that relationship at that time. No more, no less.

## WHEN LOVE MEANS MORE, NOT LESS

There might be times you may wonder about a situation where more rather than less control is the healthiest boundary to set. Consider the case of Jamie below.

As a nineteen-year-old freshman, Jamie was not doing well in his first year at college. Despite a solid high school record, reports from the academic advisory office to his parents showed that he was barely passing three of his classes, and if his grades did not improve, he was likely to go on academic probation.

This news was surprising and disturbing to Jamie's folks, who had always known their son to be a consistent and steady achiever. Their first instinct was to go to the school and check on him, but, assured by the college that early struggles are not unexpected for new students, they backed off this plan. They decided they shouldn't get too involved too soon. Plus, they wanted their son to have his college experience. Although they were worried and their inaction didn't quite feel right to them, they left the situation alone. However, a call came barely a week later, informing them that their son had been in a car wreck and they needed to get to the hospital right away.

Apparently, Jamie had been out binge drinking with some other students—including the driver, who'd passed out at the wheel. When his parents arrived, Jamie was awake and only mildly injured, with a few broken fingers and some painfully bruised ribs. After a lot of hugs and tears, the family conversation began in earnest. Jamie's parents were determined; he was not ready to be off on his own. Citing his poor academic performance and the danger of the situation he had just been in, they told him that their minds were made up. Jamie needed—and was going to get—a slower start. This meant going back home and attending community college for at least a year.

Jamie did not take the news well, viewing his parents' move as punishment and a way to keep him away from his new friends. Despite his tearful protest and pleas for them to reconsider, his parents held firm. They knew their son, and he wasn't ready. So Jamie got dragged back home kicking and screaming that very night.

Much to Jamie's surprise, within a few weeks he found that he liked being back home. Without the social pressures and the strain of learning to live on his own, he was able to focus on his classes. And when he was certain he could handle the academic workload, he took on a part-time job to help with expenses. He also rekindled an old romance. Instead of bad grades, drinking binges, and general instability, Jamie was suddenly doing well and growing.

This is prodependent love and healthy boundaries in action.

## Chapter Eight

# PRODEPENDENT RELATIONSHIPS

*One of the basic rules of the universe is that nothing is perfect.*
*Perfection simply doesn't exist. Without imperfection,*
*neither you nor I would exist.*

—Stephen Hawking

## THE LAWS OF ATTRACTION

No one gets a free ride. Whether we end up moody, depressed, shameful, intense, joyful, shy, optimistic, addicted or just plain lost we are all affected by trauma and loss. The earlier the trauma and more damaging the wounds, the more problems we face as adults, most often reflected in our intimate relationships. This is a fact. Fortunately, many of us can and do heal on our own when guided by the wisdom, insight, and emotional maturity that hopefully comes as we age.

Those of us needing more direction to improve our lives will turn to compassionate and experienced experts for guidance. This is where good psychotherapy can help remove the chains that bind us. When or if any of us choose to enter productive therapy, that process offers the opportunity to bring order, peace, direction, and acceptance into our lives. When at its best, therapy is a way to fully engage experienced, empathic adults who can guide us toward becoming better people.

Prodependence is an alternative way to view (and treat) loved ones of active addicts by offering them compassionate-validating support as opposed to insight-oriented exploration. In this sense it is unquestionably an "anti-codependency" model, as it asks the therapist to put little to no focus on our clients' early life, but rather on helping them get through a "here and now" crisis.

Prodependence discourages clinicians from "going there" at the start, if for no reason than the fact that our job one is to focus on the actual problems that brought the client to us in the first place. Part of becoming a mature therapist is to understand that not every client can, wants, or needs to spend years in therapy, nor do they want or need to resolve every issue that comes into the room. As stated, most people just want things to get better. Yes, we all have past issues that influence the present, but that doesn't mean that our lives will be unfulfilling or lacking if not investigated in therapy.

After all, there is more than one path to the same destination, therapy being just one of many. Prodependence says that a client's decision to work on past concerns after their lives have stabilized is a personal choice—not a therapist's choice. More importantly prodependence says that a therapist should never blame, shame, or leave anyone feeling that someone else's actions can ever be their fault. No one should ever take responsibility for the active problems of another adult, including adult children. We can leave people vulnerable, we can hurt them, we can let them down or rage at them, but we can never make them use or act out—period. That decision is theirs and theirs alone. This, too, differentiates codependency from prodependence as prodependence actively discourages any of us from going down the road of "what is your part in this?" Period.

Like it or not, human beings are designed to pair with people who live with similar challenges as our own. This is another research-driven fact. We are comfortable loving those we love in part because the dynamics we share with them are familiar to us from early life. This does not mean that if my mother was an addict that my spouse or child is preordained to become an addict. Nor does this mean that any of us are destined to seek out or tolerate addicted people. It simply means that we tend to lean into relationships that feel familiar, which invites both of us to heal early life, unresolved issues. The relationship dynamics that work for one couple or family might leave others running for shelter.

## I Thought I Was the Healthy One!

As I write this, I am well aware that it will leave many spouses and families feeling confused, even angry. "But this is the opposite of everything you said. You told me that the past is not driving and supporting my choice to remain with the addict. I thought there was no codependence."

And there isn't.

Many clients who are fed up with the codependency model resent the implication that they are likely to bond with people who have similar early challenges to their own. What they don't understand is that this is a good thing! Building a relationship with someone with shared or mirrored issues to our own offers both of us the chance to grow and heal together.

Dr. Marion Solomon, author of *Lean on Me*, states:

> We learn patterns of relating in early childhood and then tend to re-create them repeatedly in our lives. Indeed, most partners choose each other with the unconscious hope of repeating what was good and repairing what was bad or lacking in their earliest relationships . . . but early injury does not have to cause unhappy adult relationships. In fact, nurturing our intimate relationships in the present is the means by which emotional wounds from childhood can be healed.

Perhaps we love such people because we see the potential for us to grow together. Perhaps we love and stay with them because we can see the better, more loving person they might become. Perhaps we hold the vision of these people at their best when everyone else around them sees only the bad and not the good. How could that be a bad thing? And just like my grandma used to say, "There's a lid for every pot."

Not everyone who grew up with an alcoholic or absent parent is destined to partner with people who will eventually hurt them or become an addict themselves. Do some of us pair with addicts or other people with issues because that is a familiar dynamic? Sure. Is that an inevitable outcome for our intimate connections? No. Does everyone who bonds with and loves an addict have an extensive trauma history of their own? Maybe, maybe not.

Codependence views those who bond or remain with active addicts as if they themselves were addicted to their troubled loved one. The theory of prodependence counters this by saying that such people are more obsessed with trying to end the problem itself than they are somehow addicted to the person they love. *No one is ever addicted to another person!* Consider this—why would we ever want to pathologize a person whose "problem" is typically defined as loving too much? Is loving someone too much even possible? If so, count me in. As a healthy friend, spouse, and family member, I am grateful for all the affection and care I receive while giving away all the love I can. At last, we can say that this is the road to self-realization and achieving my potential that codependency does not offer. Prodependence asks me to celebrate our vulnerabilities together, in good times and in bad, because it is "in a relationship" and not alone where I can learn to become the best version of myself.

Undoubtedly, my love may at times be delivered in unskilled or ineffective ways. The way I love may get in the way of my own or others' healing without my seeing or knowing it. I may choose people who cannot love me back. Some of those I love may hurt or abandon me. I may end up loving the wrong people. I may end up hurting the people I love or they may hurt me. But please don't tell me that any of us can love too much. Love poorly, yes. Love inadequately, yes. Love imperfectly, yes. Love in overly needful ways, yes. Love selfishly, yes. But love too much? No way.

The story below may be helpful:

Sam grew up in a highly dysfunctional home with a mentally ill mother who was sometimes deeply loving and intelligent, and sometimes running naked down the street screaming about the people who she believed were trying to kill her. Because of this, Sam learned very early in life to continually monitor the moods of people around him and to modulate his expressions and behaviors to mitigate any "craziness" he might encounter as an adult.

And this makes perfect sense. As a child, he adapted to his unpredictable environment as a way of surviving profound family dysfunction.

When I first met Sam in therapy, he expressed frustration with his dating experiences. He put it this way: "Considering how I grew up, you'd think I would want a calm, stable partnership with none of the chaos of my childhood. But when I meet a woman like that, all I want to do is find someone else because those dates are incredibly boring. And I mean it, I'd rather date a rock. But then I meet a woman who's been in abusive relationships, struggles to keep her commitments, has lived in nine different places in five years and I'm in. I am ready for marriage that day because from the get-go, I feel like they are the perfect person. Sam, though he continually told himself (and others) that he wanted a life nothing like the life he grew up with, found himself attracted to women who provided exactly that.

Sam's frustration is not unusual for people who've grown up in dysfunctional environments. As much as Sam thinks he wants a calm and stable partner, he finds that those women have no emotional resonance for him. He is just not attuned to that type of person. When he meets an attractive woman who is open, warm, loving, and doesn't create drama on a regular basis, he struggles to relate to and connect with her or he behaves in ways that create the drama he seems to need, which of course pushes the less drama-centric woman away.

Now Sam could spend years working on his past, why he chooses such people, and how to gain more emotional resonance with health-ier people. But that experience may offer Sam little insight while he continues to date all the wrong women. What is more likely to help Sam is boundaries. After all, he already knows that the people he dates are going to have issues. He already knows that this type of person mirrors some of his past intimacies and thus this is who attracts him. Rather than working for years to (maybe, maybe not) help Sam to pick healthier partners, why not help Sam to set boundaries with the women who turn him on? Knowing what he knows about his dating habits, he recognizes that he needs to be careful about his choices. And this is where the boundaries come in. Yes, she may have issues just like his. But is she sober? Is her life stable? Does she have friends, a job, a life and a place to live? Is she in therapy? Is she mature enough to take responsibility for her own actions? You see Sam can't help who he is attracted to. It is what it is. But having this awareness, plus healthy boundaries related to who he will see and who he will not, is the likely path to his finding healthy love and family. Not fixing here, but adapting.

## BIRDS OF A FEATHER . . .

A highly useful way to understand what Sam is going through is to consider the process of filial imprinting in birds. Filial imprinting occurs when a bird imprints on a parent and follows and mimics the actions of that parent. (Think about chicks following a hen, or gos-lings following a goose.) Filial imprinting in birds gives them a sense of species identification. They do not automatically know what they are when they hatch, so they visually imprint on their parents, and then they identify with their species for life.

That is the ideal version of filial imprinting in birds. But some birds will imprint on humans. Ornithologist Konrad Lorenz found that incubator-hatched geese will imprint on the first moving stimulus they see after hatching. For example, Lorenz had geese imprinted on him—or, more specifically, his wading boots. (He is often described as having a gaggle of geese following him around his lab—as both goslings and adults because geese imprint for life.) Lorenz even got a batch of geese to imprint on a colorful box placed on a model train, which they followed as it circled its track.

Humans, of course, are far more emotionally sophisticated than chicks and goslings, but the concept of filial imprinting nonetheless holds water. Birds imprint on the physical manifestations of whatever they see immediately after birth. Humans attune similarly, but to more than just the first thing we see. We also imprint on powerful emotional experiences. As infants, toddlers, and children, we learn what it means to be taken care of, to feel stimulated, to be engaged, to be validated, to be comforted, to be ignored, and all the rest. And we carry that imprint with us in our adult lives—seeking relationships that evoke this imprint even if we intellectually might prefer something else.

So, as stated earlier, we find people we can relate to and feel comfortable with, those whose dysfunction mirrors or meshes with our own. We do this because these are the people with whom we can emotionally and psychologically connect, and, ideally, with whom we can emotionally and psychologically grow. As long as we share the values of honesty, integrity and a willingness to take responsibility for their part in our problems we are right for one another. And when problems do occur, as they inevitably will, we both agree to seek help to get our relationship back on track.

## IMPRINTING IN THE CODEPENDENCE CONTEXT

The codependency model recognizes the fact that we seek what we know, that we imprint emotionally and seek to bond with "our species" as we grow into adults. However, instead of celebrating the fact that two emotional equivalents have come together in a relationship where both can grow, codependence labels non-addicted loved ones as emotionally troubled for having partnered with people who are addicted.

What codependence fails to acknowledge is that people tend to come together because they can relate to and connect with one another on a level that is comfortable and familiar. And usually two people will naturally stay at the same emotional and psychological level or move up or down the scale slightly over time, which enables them to continue relating to and staying connected with one another.

> What codependence fails to acknowledge is that people tend to come together because they can relate to and connect with one another on a level that is comfortable and familiar.

The good news is that if both parties in a relationship are willing to grow and do the work, such issues can be overcome.

## IMPRINTING IN THE PRODEPENDENCE CONTEXT

Prodependent relationships are a matter of finding the partner that fits us best, and, when necessary, growing over time with that partner. This is a far cry from the "detach with love" advice we tend to hear with codependence. Detach with love typically means that we work on ourselves and leave our addicted loved one to their own devices. When reframed using the prodependence model, however, we can happily and healthfully do what comes naturally to us as human beings. We can continue to love and support the addict, but in ways that are more helpful to the addict, while doing a better job of making sure our own needs are met. If the addict is willing to grow as we grow, there is hope.

Like it or not, the dynamics of love and connection that we experience and learn in childhood from our parents affect our later-life relationship choices, as well as how we behave within those relationships. This is neither good nor bad, right nor wrong. It just is.

Viewing life through the lens of prodependence, partners of addicts can say:

- Maybe it's not true that I'm partnered with the wrong person and that's why I'm unhappy.
- Maybe it's not true that I'm doomed to only spend time with losers.
- Maybe we are better off growing together than apart from one another.
- Maybe the attachment I feel to my addicted loved one is not crazy or unhealthy, but an opportunity to grow.
- Maybe I'm not messed up to the point where I can never have healthy relationships. I just need to make more informed choices, balancing my heart and my head.

We are all wounded in one way or another. No one makes it to adult life without some well-earned emotional and psychological battle scars. Some of us have more scars than others, of course. And that's okay. It doesn't mean we're inherently broken or unlovable; it simply means we are more likely to bond with people who are similarly wounded because *these are our people*. We get them, we understand them, we can relate to them, and they to us. We provide and can tolerate (and even thrive in) one another's challenges.

> We are all wounded in one way or another. No one makes it to adult life without some well-earned emotional and psychological battle scars. Some of us have more scars than others, of course. And that's okay. It doesn't mean we're inherently broken or unlovable; it simply means we are more likely to bond with people who are similarly wounded because *these are our people.*

Who cares if we found each other at the scratch-and-dent sale? We found each other. And we connected. Now you are providing me with the polish I needed for so long, as I'm doing for you. And now, even if it's only because addiction is forcing us to do so, we can grow and become emotionally healthier together. Because we fit. Our relationship is and can continue to be mutually beneficial, with one person's strengths filling in the weak points of the other, and vice versa. Even when our strengths and weaknesses evolve over time. This is the essence of healthy interdependency.

## PRODEPENDENCE IS NOT ONE SIZE FITS ALL

Healthy human attachment does not look the same for every person. It differs, sometimes quite a lot, based on not just trauma, but genetics, social background, technological fluency, and gender, among other factors.

- **Genetics**. The impact of genetics on personality, especially on aspects of connection, attachment, and dependence, is not well

understood. We do, however, know that certain inheritable personality traits affect a person's behavior, including issues such
as impulsivity[1] and susceptibility to emotional and psychological issues such as depression,[2] anxiety,[3] and addiction.[4] At the
very least, these well-established genetic traits can influence a
person's comfort level with connection, attachment, and dependence, potentially altering that person's comfort zone on the
spectrum of dependency.

- **Social Background.** The explicit and implicit lessons learned
  from parents, religion, racial and ethnic background, and general social milieu affect a person's ability to relate to and connect with others throughout life. For example, a person may
  have been raised in a perfectly loving and supportive home
  where affection was not openly displayed. If so, that individual
  may choose to display affection and attachment less openly
  and comfortably than a person raised in a more demonstrative
  environment.

- **Reliance on and Fluency with Technology.** As little as a few
  years ago, I would not have listed technology as impacting a
  person's comfort level with attachment. In our increasingly
  digital world, however, meaningful connection and the provi-
  sion of support can look very different for different people. For
  example, for younger individuals, online connections can be
  (and often are) as emotionally impactful as real-world interactions, while older individuals typically don't experience that.
  Either way, the use of technology can affect the way in which
  a person experiences attachment. Some people will use tech to
  feel connected, appreciated, supported, and loved, while others

will use it as a buffer that helps them interact without becoming vulnerable (and, therefore, without developing true intimacy).

- **Gender.** In a general way, women tend to be more empathetic and community-based than men, with men being more analytical and willing to go it alone than women. Because of these basic differences, men's comfort levels with intimate attachment tend to be slightly lower.

The point I am making here is that not everyone can or should try to become what might appear to a casual observer to be "emotionally healthy." Emotional health is highly subjective, depending on the individual. What looks like an emotional three to you might look like an emotional ten to me, and that's the way it is.

We are who we are. Sure, we can tinker at the edges and slowly make healthy progress, learning to behave in ways that better serve us and our loved ones, but we cannot change our essential selves. If we're skittish about attachment, so be it, as long as we're not completely alone and isolated in ways that leave us feeling bereft and unsupported. If we're naturally a caregiver, that's great, as long as we're not overdoing it and stifling or smothering the people we care for.

At the end of the day, healthy emotional connection—prodependence—looks different for every person and every relationship. Recognizing this, it is important for therapists, especially early in the healing process, to meet clients where they are, including their comfort level with attachment. From that starting point, we can help them work their way toward prodependence, whatever that might look like for them. Along the way, clients and their loved ones can continue to fill in each other's weak spots in ways that are healthy for them.

# A SUMMARY OF PRODEPENDENCE

Like addicts, loved ones of addicts typically have (occasionally extensive) trauma histories. It's not unusual, in fact, for all those concerned to have experienced some form of past trauma. But for those who love the addict, trauma hasn't completely poisoned the well of attachment, which is why they keep trying to help and to connect with them. It's also why trying to apply a trauma-based model of healing to loved ones of addicts tends to get wonky.

For caregiving loved ones of addicts, attachment is desirable and important. No matter how badly they've been traumatized, they're still reaching out and trying to connect. They may be doing this in unhelpful ways because that's what their early-life family dysfunction and trauma taught them to do, but they're still trying. And telling them they're traumatized and damaged and making bad decisions and entering bad relationships and staying in bad relationships because they're messed up by trauma, does not help them or give them a sense of hope. Instead, it feels like blaming and shaming, and it tends to drive them away from the help they need.

> For caregiving loved ones of addicts, attachment is desirable and important. No matter how badly they've been traumatized, they're still reaching out and trying to connect.

Addicts need their bad behavior and its underlying causes brought into the light. Addicts need their denial about what they're doing, why they're doing it, and the problems this is causing to be shattered. Caregiving loved ones of addicts? Not so much. Instead of confrontation and giant doses of reality, they need validation, loving support, and guidance for moving forward in ways that don't enmesh, enable, or control.

Talking to loved ones early in the healing process about things like early life trauma and how that's affecting their present-day behaviors is not an effective tactic. We need a different approach with caregiving loved ones—a treatment model that recognizes and celebrates their desire and need for attachment as a strength they can use for healing.

That model is prodependence.

Once again, this does not mean that loved ones of addicts don't have their own struggles based in trauma. They do. But trauma is not what causes them to stay with the addict or to caretake the addict.

So, instead of pointing out their trauma and how it pushes them into unhealthy behaviors, we need to put our arms around them and commiserate while giving them tools for self-care, better boundaries, and healthier relating. Yes, we do need to identify and acknowledge the trauma wrought by the addiction. But digging deeper into a caregiving loved one's history in the early stages of healing is counterproductive. Caregivers don't respond to this because they're not ready to hear about it or deal with it. That's just not where they are. If we approach these individuals from an attachment perspective, where we affirm them and validate them, however, they tend to respond positively. They stick around, they do the work, they make changes and they heal. With the attachment-based prodependence model we, as therapists, can do a significant amount of desperately needed behaviorally focused crisis and intervention work without forcing loved ones into deeper issues before they are ready.

## What About the Addict?
## Codependence vs. Prodependence

Codependence implicitly tells addicts the following: "If the people who love you had just been healthier, more insightful, and *just plain less codependent,* they would have walked away from you a long time ago." Or worse, "If your spouse/partner had grown up with less trauma, they never would have chosen you in the first place." And, saving the worst for last, "Once the people who love you most have recognized and worked on their codependency, they may not want to remain in relationship with someone as troubled as you." And I gotta tell you, that is a message that would keep me drinking and acting out as it implies to the addict, "You are too sick to be loved by anyone healthy enough to leave you."

Think for a moment how that message would be interpreted by the newly recovering addict. To them, it simply says, "As your loved ones heal from their codependency, they will more clearly see how you have harmed their lives. So, if you want them to stay around, you'd better fix yourself quickly and in the right way—or surely, they will kick you to the curb." Prodependence, by carrying a message of strength and hope, sends addicts a completely different message. What prodependence says about those who still actively care about the addict is the following: "Despite all you have done, they stuck around when others might have simply gone away. Maybe, just maybe, they stayed around because they can still see the good in you that they are certain will return if you get sober."

The crux of this message offers a whole lot more hope for the future of all concerned than that of codependence. Implicit in this prodependent theme for the addict is this message: "No matter how badly you feel about they way you've lived, those who know and love you best have stuck around because they still see the good inside you. They are holding on to the person they love that the addiction has shoved aside."

This redemptive view of addiction is part of the game-changer that prodependence brings. Telling addicts that despite their problems or those they have caused others, that they remain good people who are deserving of love is exactly the right message needed to inspire recovery. In treatment, as in life, themes of hope and love will always resonate more strongly than do those that imply deserved abandonment.

## A FINAL WORD

When treating loved ones of addicts, we can approach them from love or fear. Prodependence comes from love, love, and more love. Just as the caregiver comes from love. More importantly, prodependence meets the caregiver where they are using language and concepts that they can readily understand and identify with. And it does this with empathy, concern, boundaries, support, hope, and concrete direction.

# Definitions and FAQs

**Q:** Why change things? What was wrong with codependence?

**A:** I wrote this book because I have seen too many addicts' loved ones turn away from desperately needed direction and support because they couldn't or wouldn't accept the codependence tenet that being in this situation automatically implies there is something wrong with them. Meanwhile, their chronically addicted partner, parent, or child is failing at school, getting fired from another job, or getting arrested. I have seen many good therapists lacking useful answers to help such family members and caregivers. Often, the therapist's only choice is to rely on models such as codependence, which feels more negative and alienating than invitational. From a professional lens, we cannot continue to embrace codependency as the concept has not been backed up by validated research, has never been a formal diagnosis and is biased against both gender and culture. Additionally, the theory of codependence has never been formalized as a clinical diagnosis because we have been unable to validate the theory via clinical research. In fact, the concept was reviewed proposed and rejected by the American Psychiatric Association on multiple occasions.

Q: **What is the major difference between codependence and prodependence?**

A: **Codependence** is a trauma-based theory of human dependency which, by definition, states that those who partner with or are active caregivers of addicts do so as a form of trauma repetition—putting themselves in a relationship where the other person's needs will eventually exceed and overwhelm their own. These caretakers, by definition, demonstrate their trauma-based low self-esteem and desperate desire for approval by seeking out and becoming deeply attached to such troubled people, feeling that they can resolve the addict's problems. As such it is based in both psychoanalytic and trauma theory. To "be codependent" implies that one tends to bond deeply with those with whom interactions often mirror early traumatic deficits. Failure on the part of the active addict then serves as a trigger for the nonaddicted partner to act out their unmet needs or abuse from childhood within this troubled adult relationship. Codependence implies that the loved ones of addicts, due to their underlying, often unconscious "childhood issues" tend to, as adults, give too much and love too much. Thus, they attract, enable, and enmesh with addicts. The goals of codependency treatment revolve around themes of detachment, self-actualization, becoming less needy, and working through past trauma to become more aware, less enabling, and less accepting of troubled, emotionally unavailable people.

**Prodependence** is a strength-based, attachment-based theory of human dependency which, by definition, states that those who partner or deeply give of themselves to an active addict are no more than loving people caught up in circumstances beyond their ability to healthfully cope. As such, they are viewed as people in the midst of a profound life crisis, one which they cannot resolve despite their best efforts to do so  Moreover, their desire to help the addict and all related actions toward helping the addict demonstrate nothing more than a normal and healthy attempt to remain connected to a failing loved one while facing extraordinarily difficult circumstances. Prodependence says that it is a gift for us to bond with people at a similar level of emotional functioning as our own because this offers the greatest opportunity for growth. To "be prodependent" implies that one is able to create deep, bonded adult attachments that mirror our very human, normative longings for healthy dependence and intimacy. Prodependence assumes that, when one loves and bonds deeply, it is natural and therefore non-pathological to do whatever it takes to ensure the safety and stability of those with whom one is attached. Prodependence implies that loved ones of addicts will understandably take extraordinary measures to keep those they love stable and to ensure their safety. There is no pathology assigned to loving in prodependence. Rather, prodependence asserts that loving addicts or other chronically troubled people healthfully requires a different form of love than that with healthy adults. Loving prodependently requires support, guidance, and informed help.

Q: **When did codependence evolve into theory and practice?**

A: Codependence was initially promoted in six books published between 1981 and 1989, mostly written by female therapists who worked in the addiction field. It meshed with and ultimately subsumed the preexisting co-addiction movement. And later it broadened in the larger culture to include caregivers of all stripes, not just caregivers of addicts.

**Q:** **Why did codependence become so popular?**

**A:** Codependence was an easy-to-understand, engaging concept, and that profoundly mirrored the culture of the era of its creation.

**Q:** **Can codependence treatment be counterproductive when working with loved ones of addicts?**

**A:** Yes, and it frequently is. Codependence, by definition, implies that there is something wrong with the person who loves, rescues, helps, and cares for an addict. This is especially true if that person has given up essential parts of themselves in the process. Embracing the codependence model requires loved ones of addicts, who are already in crisis, to accept that there is something wrong with them that they need to fix. This can lead to caregivers feeling misunderstood and judged. As a result, many leave treatment before they receive the help they desperately need.

**Q:** **Is this book suggesting that codependency doesn't exist as a mental health or addiction diagnosis?**

**A:** Yes. Prodependence, as a concept and in practice, does not support the concept of codependence as form of legitimate assessment, diagnosis, or therapy. Prodependence sees codependence as a pop-culture concept that does not fully encompass the lived experience of addicts' loved ones, nor take into account the needs of the situations they face. Execution of the codependence model in treatment can often alienate the people it was designed to help, as it leaves them feeling more judged than supported.

Q: **How does prodependence view the problem behaviors acted out by an addict's loved ones, such as enabling, overzealously caretaking, and even raging at the addict?**

A: Prodependence views all such activity as the caregiver's "best attempt" to save a troubled loved one. It sees these behaviors as loving—though often less than ideal—efforts to save a person they care for. These behaviors are viewed as problematic only due to their ineffectiveness and potential to escalate the problems they were intended to solve. However, prodependence does not label or judge the loved one who engages in such behaviors. Instead, prodependence views these actions as a loved one's best effort to stay connected and help in a situation that is far beyond their ability to remedy.

Q: **How does prodependence tackle typical challenges to treating loved ones of addicts, including emotional reactivity and enabling?**

A: Prodependence considers the fact that loved ones usually lack the specialized training or education that would equip them to work with an out-of-control, addicted person. After all, most people did not study addiction treatment in high school. Prodependence also recognizes the immense pain and fear that comes along with witnessing a beloved family member fail. These individuals often compensate for their lack of expertise with passionate attempts to help their loved one, but, because of the lack of proper training, their efforts are often not useful and can at times be unintentionally counterproductive. The prodependent therapist does not pathologize family members' attempts to heal someone they love. They are not regarded as anything but loving, even when their attempts fail. The goal here is to support family members through the crisis wrought by addiction by validating their love while simultaneously helping them develop more effective coping skills.

Q: **Does prodependence say that there is nothing wrong with the loved ones of an addict, even when they exhibit problematic traits?**

A: Prodependence implies that such loved ones of addicts are caught up in circumstances, such as witnessing the emotional decline of a beloved family member, that would naturally overwhelm anyone. Thus, there is nothing "wrong" with them, in terms of relating to the addict, regardless of their personal history. They are trying as best they can to survive a profound life crisis by trying to help their loved ones survive extraordinary, overwhelming circumstances. What these caregivers require from early treatment is validation for the love and care they have given, in addition to supportive and clear directions about loving their troubled family member in healthier ways. That said, loved ones of addicts may in fact have underlying trauma and other issues that they might eventually want to address. (See the next three questions for more on this topic.)

Q: **What about trauma? Don't many spouses and family members of addicts have early childhood trauma?**

A. Yes, many of us who love addicts, much like addicts themselves, have had early or later-life traumatic experiences. In fact, these similar histories, both conscious and unconscious, are frequently part of what has bonded these people to one another. And some loved ones in crisis may act out elements of their own past trauma in the acute stages of the addict's problems. This is unsurprising, considering the extremely stressful and overwhelming circumstances addictions produce. That said, many people who are deeply attached to addicts and alcoholics lack any traumatic history of their own. Either way, initial therapy and treatment for such people, utilizing the prodependence model, does not seek to investigate or treat such issues. Instead, the intention is to address the problems that these partners are currently attempting to solve.

Q. **How does prodependence view and treat past trauma in partners of addicts?**

A. Prodependence views the close caregiver of an addict as themselves being in crisis from the very start of treatment. Therefore, all their care is intended to help them adapt to and resolve their immediate crisis. After the crisis of active addiction has been resolved, the client may be interested or encouraged to examine their personal history. However, prodependence does not bind the reactions of someone involved with an active addict to their past. Asking a loved one to address early trauma—or even to examine their own history—early in the recovery is experienced as more hurtful than helpful as doing so implies an innate fault with the caregiver.

Q. **What happens when a loved one who is involved with an alcoholic or addict appears so emotionally disabled that**

**they are actively interfering with the process of healing the addiction?**

A: If the loved one is unable to be soothed, supported, or redirected in early addiction treatment, this simply implies that they need care that is separate and apart from their relationship with the addict. These are often familiar and diagnosable conditions—exhibited as a result of living under profound stress—such as depression, anxiety, or the triggering of past traumatic events. As these individuals heal, their treatment can then be integrated into overall addiction family care.

Q: **What about the apparent desire of "codependent" people, in general, to self-actualize and grow, independent of their relationships and bonds?**

A: Prodependence, coming from an attachment-based perspective, says that all of us are deeply dependent on one another for emotional survival and, further, that this is a good thing. Mutual, deep, and enduring dependencies from womb to tomb is how humans survive and thrive; as such, relationships should never be regarded as inherently pathological. Prodependence celebrates rather than pathologizes deep emotional dependency. It regards healthy, deeply bonded relationships of all kinds as key to an individual's self-actualization. Enmeshment is viewed merely as an inadequate attempt at loving. An individual practicing enmeshment requires new skills to improve their relationships. Prodependence says that we are all individuals who make our own choices when out in the world as best we can but that the foundation of our lives must rest on the depth or our interpersonal relationships.

Q: What about those who are so needy and desperate in close relationships that they become unable to function without one? Aren't they deeply codependent?

A: For several decades, the *Diagnostic and Statistical Manual of Mental Disorders* has had a fully fleshed out, criteria-based diagnosis for people who are so emotionally limited and impaired that they "cling" to other people for their own emotional stability. It's called Dependent Personality Disorder. Sadly, DPD and codependence have become conflated.

Q: What kind of treatment should be offered to loved ones of addicts? Don't they still need help with boundaries, self-care, and managing their situations?

A: Any loving person in a meaningful relationship with an active addict is, by definition, in need of support. They likely need encouragement toward both greater self-care and establishing healthy boundaries with their troubled loved one. Many such people simply need help with the addiction-related crises they experience near daily. However, no loving person in a meaningful relationship with an active addict should be asked to doubt the nature of their love or to question their own emotional stability in order to be taught such skills and to be given the support that they deserve.

Q: What do you say to the millions of people who have embraced the concept of codependence? Where does prodependence leave these individuals?

A: Taking the path of self-exploration and personal growth is a positive thing that strengthens individuals and society. I am certain that many of those who have embraced codependence have become better people for having done so; that is to be applauded. I would simply ask such individuals to reconsider the concept of "loving too much," as I think the phrase is demeaning. For example, you may love in the wrong ways for the wrong reasons. You may love in ways that don't achieve the result you seek. You may love and lose. You may love and hurt. However, you can never feel too much love, express too much compassion, or exhibit too much empathy. Claiming this is possible is counterintuitive to the realities of healthy human attachment and bonding. In fact, deepening intimacy with our partners and family members allows all of us to achieve a higher form of self-actualization than is otherwise possible.

# Endnotes

## Preface

1 Darwin, C. (1909). *The origin of species*. Dent.

## Chapter 3

1 Tupac Shakur, *Tupac: Resurrection* 1971-1996. https://www.biblio. com/book/tupac-resurrection-1971-1996-tupac-shakur/d/138050 8155?aid=frg&gclid=Cj0KCQjw0umSBhDrARIsAH7FCocE87mZ x71p_GQue_J1ng83MvzifYqaB3M2EcVxlqi4R71m-clvqQ0aAoT-bEALw_wcB.

2 Greening, T. (2006). Five basic postulates of humanistic psychology. *Journal of Humanistic Psychology, 46*(3), 239–239.

3 Courtois, C. A. (2014). *It's not you, it's what happened to you: Complex trauma and treatment*. Telemachus Press.

4 Courtois, C. A. (2014). *It's not you, it's what happened to you: Complex trauma and treatment*. Telemachus Press.

5 Anda, R., Felitti, V., Bremner, J., Walker, J., Whitfield, C., Perry, B., . . . Giles, W. (2006). The enduring effects of abuse and related adverse

experiences in childhood. *European Archives of Psychiatry and Clinical Neuroscience,* 256(3), 174–186.

6  Beattie, M. (1992). *Codependent no more: How to stop controlling others and start caring for yourself.* Hazelden Publishing.

7  Jackson, J. (1962). Alcoholism and the family. In D. Pittman & C. Snyder (Eds.), *Society, Culture and Drinking Patterns,* pp. 472–492. New York: John Wiley & Sons; and, Chaudron, C. D. & Wilkinson, D. A., Eds. (1988). *Theories on alcoholism.* Addiction Research Foundation, pp. 297–298.

8  White, W., & Savage, B. (2005). All in the family: Alcohol and other drug problems, recovery, advocacy. *Alcoholism Treatment Quarterly,* 23(4), 3–37, citing Day, B. (1961). Alcoholism and the family. *Marriage and Family Living,* 23, 253–258, and, Reddy, B. (1971). The family disease—alcoholism. Unpublished Manuscript.

### Chapter 4

1  Webster, M. (2006). Merriam-Webster online dictionary.

2  Cottrell, L. S., & Gallagher, R. (1941). Important developments in American social psychology during the past decade. Sociometry, 4(2), 107–139.

3  Alcoholics Anonymous, "AA Timeline," http://www.aa.org/pages/en_US/aa-timeline.

4  White, W. (2015). The vulnerability and resilience of children affected by addiction: Career reflections of Dr. Claudia Black, www.williamwhitepapers.com; and, Adult Children of Alcoholics (undated). Adult Children of Alcoholics and its Beginnings, http://www.adultchildren.org/lit-EarlyHistory.

5  Black, C. (1981). *It Will Never Happen to Me: Children of Alcoholics as Youngsters—adolescents—adults.* Ballantine Books.

6  Woititz, J. G. (1990). *Adult children of alcoholics: expanded edition.* Health Communications, Inc.

7  Norwood, R. (1986). *Women who love too much: When you keep wishing and hoping he'll change.* Simon and Schuster.

8  Cermak, T. L. (1986). *Diagnosing and treating co-dependence: A guide for professionals who work with chemical dependents, their spouses and children.* Johnson Institute Books.

9  Beattie, M. (1986). *Codependent no more: How to stop controlling others and start caring for yourself.* Hazelden.

10  Mellody, P., Miller, A. W., & Miller, J. K. (1989). *Facing codependence: What it is, where it comes from, how it sabotages our lives.* HarperCollins.

11  Beattie, M. (1986). *Codependent no more: How to stop controlling others and start caring for yourself.* Hazelden.

12  Cermak, T. L. (1986). Diagnostic criteria for codependency. *Journal of psychoactive drugs,* 18(1), 15–20.

13  Irvine, L. (1999). *Codependent forevermore: The invention of self in a twelve-step group.* University of Chicago Press.

14  American Psychiatric Association. (2013). *Diagnostic and statistical manual of mental disorders (DSM-5®).* American Psychiatric Pub.

15  American Psychiatric Association. (2013). *Diagnostic and statistical manual of mental disorders (DSM-5®).* American Psychiatric Pub.

16  Wikipedia. Dependent Personality Disorder. Retrieved Mar 8, 2018 from https:// en.wikipedia.org/wiki/Dependent personality disorder.

17  Beattie, M. (1992). *Codependent no more: How to stop controlling others and start caring for yourself.* Hazelden Publishing.

18  Rosenberg, R.A. (2018). *The human magnet syndrome: The codependent narcissist trap.* CreateSpace Independent Publishing.

19  Rosenberg, R. (2013). The History of the Term Codependency. https://blogs.psych central.com/human-magnets/2013/11/the-history-of-the-term-codependency/.

20  Beattie, M. (1992). *Codependent no more: How to stop controlling others and start caring for yourself.* Hazelden Publishing.

21  Beattie, M. (1992). *Codependent no more: How to stop controlling others and start caring for yourself.* Hazelden Publishing.

22  Cowan, G., & Warren, L. W. (1994). Codependency and gender-stereotyped traits. *Sex Roles, 30*(9), 631–645.

23  Schaef, A. W. (1986). *Codependence: Misunderstood-mistreated.* HarperCollins.

24  *The Therapist* (2020). Understanding mental health stigma in Black and Latinx/Hispanic communities: An interview with Marianne Diaz and Eric Katende. *The Therapist, 2020*, 16–19.

**Chapter 5**

1  Johnson, S. (2013). *Love sense: The revolutionary new science of romantic relationships.* Little, Brown.

2  Saah, T. (2005). The evolutionary origins and significance of drug addiction. *Harm reduction journal, 2*(1), 8.

3  Maté, G. (2010). *In the realm of hungry ghosts: Close encounters with addiction.* North Atlantic Books.

4   Hawkley, L. C., Masi, C. M., Berry, J. D., & Cacioppo, J. T. (2006). Loneliness is a unique predictor of age-related differences in systolic blood pressure. *Psychology and Aging*, 21(1), 152; House, J. S., Landis, K. R., & Umberson, D. (1988). Social relationships and health. *Science*, 241(4865), 540; Kiecolt-Glaser, J. K., Malarkey, W. B., Chee, M., Newton, T., Cacioppo, J. T., Mao, H. Y., & Glaser, R. (1993). Negative behavior during marital conflict is associated with immunological down-regulation; *Psychosomatic Medicine*, 55(5), 395–409; Caspi, A., Harrington, H., Moffitt, T. E., Milne, B. J., & Poulton, R. (2006). Socially isolated children 20 years later: Risk of cardiovascular disease. *Archives of Pediatrics & Adolescent Medicine*, 160(8), 805– 811; Thurston, R. C., & Kubzansky, L. D. (2009). Women, loneliness, and incident coronary heart disease. *Psychosomatic Medicine*, 71(8), 836; Hawkley, L. C., Masi, C. M., Berry, J. D., & Cacioppo, J. T. (2006). Loneliness is a unique predictor of age-related differences in systolic blood pressure. *Psychology and Aging*, 21(1), 152; Hawkley, L. C., Thisted, R. A., Masi, C. M., & Cacioppo, J. T. (2010). Loneliness predicts increased blood pressure: 5-year cross-lagged analyses in middle-aged and older adults. *Psychology and Aging*, 25(1), 132; among other studies.

5   Vaillant, G. E. (2008). *Aging well: Surprising guideposts to a happier life from the landmark study of adult development.* Little, Brown; Johnson, S. (2008). *Hold me tight: Seven conversations for a lifetime of love*, p. 26. Little, Brown.

6   Coyne, J. C., Rohrbaugh, M. J., Shoham, V., Sonnega, J. S., Nicklas, J. M., & Cranford, J. A. (2001). Prognostic importance of marital quality for survival of congestive heart failure. *The American Journal of Cardiology*, 88(5), 526–529; Luo, Y., Hawkley, L. C., Waite, L. J.,

& Cacioppo, J. T. (2012). Loneliness, health, and mortality in old age: A national longitudinal study. *Social Science & Medicine*, 74(6), 907–914; Holt-Lunstad, J., Smith, T. B., & Layton, J. B. (2010). Social relationships and mortality risk: a meta- analytic review. *PLoS Medicine*, 7(7), e1000316; Patterson, A. C., & Veenstra, G. (2010). Loneliness and risk of mortality: A longitudinal investigation in Alameda County, California. *Social Science & Medicine*, 71(1), 181–186; Perissinotto, C. M., Cenzer, I. S., & Covinsky, K. E. (2012). Loneliness in older persons: a predictor of functional decline and death. *Archives of Internal Medicine*, 172(14), 1078–1084; among other studies.

7  Ibid.

8  Bowlby, J. (1991). *Attachment and Loss (Vol. 1)*. London: Penguin Books.

9  Spock, B. (1946). *The commonsense book of baby and child care*. New York: Duell, Sloan and Pearce.

10  Ainsworth, M. D. S., Blehar, M. C., Waters, E., & Wall, S. N. (2015). *Patterns of attachment: A psychological study of the strange situation*. Psychology Press.

11  Harlow, H. F. (1958). The nature of love. *American Psychologist*, 13(12), 673.

12  Hawkley, L. C., Masi, C. M., Berry, J. D., & Cacioppo, J. T. (2006). Loneliness is a unique predictor of age-related differences in systolic blood pressure. *Psychology and Aging*, 21(1), 152.

13  Coyne, J. C., Rohrbaugh, M. J., Shoham, V., Sonnega, J. S., Nicklas, J. M., & Cranford, J. A. (2001). Prognostic importance of marital quality for survival of congestive heart failure. *The American Journal of Cardiology*, 88(5), 526–529.

14 Kiecolt-Glaser, J. K., Newton, T., Cacioppo, J. T., MacCallum, R. C., Glaser, R., & Malarkey, W. B. (1996). Marital conflict and endocrine function: Are men really more physiologically affected than women? *Journal of Consulting and Clinical Psychology*, 64(2), 324.

15 Cohen, S. (2001). Social relationships and susceptibility to the common cold. *Emotion, Social Relationships, and Health*, 221–223, and, Cohen, S., Doyle, W. J., Skoner, D. P., Rabin, B. S., & Gwaltney, J. M. (1997). Social ties and susceptibility to the common cold. *Jama*, 277(24), 1940–1944, x.

16 Pekovic, V., Seff, L., & Rothman, M. (2007). Planning for and responding to special needs of elders in natural disasters. *Generations*, 31(4), 37–41; and, Semenza, J. C., Rubin, C. H., Falter, K. H., Selanikio, J. D., Flanders, W. D., Howe, H. L., & Wilhelm, J. L. (1996). Heat-related deaths during the July 1995 heat wave in Chicago. *New England Journal of Medicine*, 335(2), 84–90.

17 House, J. S. (2001). Social isolation kills, but how and why? *Psychosomatic Medicine*, 63(2), 273–274.

18 Johnson, S. (2008). *Hold me tight: Seven conversations for a lifetime of love*. Little, Brown.

## Chapter 6

1 Bejerot, N. (1980). Addiction to pleasure: A biological and social-psychological theory of addiction. *NIDA Research Monograph*, 30, 246.

2 US Department of Health and Human Services. (2009). Results from the 2007 National Survey on Drug Use and Health: Detailed Tables. *Substance Abuse and Mental Health Services Administration. SAMHSA, Office of Applied Studies*.

3  Alexander, B. K., Beyerstein, B. L., Hadaway, P. F., & Coambs, R. B. (1981). Effect of early and later colony housing on oral ingestion of morphine in rats. *Pharmacology Biochemistry and Behavior*, 15(4), 571–576.

4  Maté, G. (2010*). In the realm of hungry ghosts: Close encounters with addiction.* North Atlantic Books.

5  Hughes, C. E., & Stevens, A. (2010). What can we learn from the Portuguese decriminalization of illicit drugs? *British Journal of Criminology*, Information retrieved from https://doi.org/10.1093/bjc/azq038.

## Chapter 7

1  McGreevy, B. (2013). *Hemlock Grove*. FSG Originals.

2  Adapted from Crisis Management by Dr. Jeffery https://www.icisf.org/wp-content/uploads/2013/04/Crisis-Intervention-and-Critical-Incident-Stress-Management-a-defense-of-the-field.pdf.

3  Mays, M. *No Man's Land, Part I*. Retrieved Oct 5, 2017 from https://partnerhope.com/2017/06/no-mans-land-part-i/; and Mays, M. *No Man's Land, Part II*. Retrieved Oct 5, 2017 from https://partnerhope.com/2017/07/weathering-no-mans-land-part-2/.

## Chapter 8

1  Anokhin, A. P., Grant, J. D., Mulligan, R. C., & Heath, A. C. (2015). The genetics of impulsivity: evidence for the heritability of delay discounting. Biological psychiatry, 77(10), 887–894.

2  Levinson, D. F. (2006). The genetics of depression: a review. Biological psychiatry, 60(2), 84–92.

3  Maier, W. (2003). Genetics of anxiety. Medical psychiatry, 21, 189–206.

4  Gelernter, J., & Kranzler, H. R. (2008). Genetics of addiction. The American psychiatric publishing textbook of substance abuse treatment, 17–27; Alsakaf, I., & Bhatia, S. C. (2017). Genetics of Addiction. Substance and Nonsubstance Related Addiction Disorder: Diagnosis and Treatment, 21; among other sources.

# Index

## A

abandonment issues, 4

accountability, 12

addiction,

    disease model of, 40, 42, 48, 64, 69, 92, 94

    dopamine and, 70

    equals isolation, 85–87

    externalizing your, 17

    as family disease, 5

    as an intimacy disorder, 85–98

    pleasure as primary driver of, 88

    as shameful, 5

    stigma of, 4–6, 7

    as symptom of trauma, 92–96

    thrives in isolation, 87–88

    unresolved early-life trauma and, 94

    viewed as moral failing, 4, 69

addictive cycle, 70

addicts,

    behaviors, importance of, 11

    caregivers of, 17

    denial, 11, 12

    dysfunctional lessons learned in childhood, 91

    feelings, wants, and needs, 11

    interdependent relations of, 17

    intimate connections and, 115–116

adrenaline, 70. See also addictive cycle

American Psychiatric Association (APA), 54, 148

anhedonia, 34

anxiety, 20, 24, 28, 34, 35, 36, 49, 70, 78, 86, 110, 124, 142, 156

attachment,

    and emotional well-being, 72–76

    genetics and, 141–142

    healthy, 2, 18

    meaningful, 17

    reliance on and fluency with technology and, 142

    secure, 76–78

    secure versus insecure, 78–79

    social background and, 142–143

    styles, 75–76

    theory (theories), ii, xv, 72, 74, 75, 149

    trauma and, 93

**B**

"be where the client is," 9

blame, 5, 6, 7, 8, 16, 17, 19, 20, 27, 43,
        46, 65, 66, 68, 107, 109, 121, 133

bonding,

    caregiving as indication of, 4

    healthy, 156

    interpersonal, 71

    intimate and secure, 75

    pair-, 108

    social, 100

boredom, 28, 70

boundaries, ii, 19, 22, 28, 58, 59, 68,
        107, 111, 113, 115, 119, 122–
        126, 127, 128, 129, 137, 145,
        146, 147, 157,

**C**

caregivers' needs, 116–117

chronic health problems, 20

codependence, 50

    arguments against diagnosis of,
        50–53

    definition of, 45

    Dependent Personality Disorder
        (DPD) and, 53–54, 55

    DSM-based psychiatric diagnosis
        for, 49

    imprinting and, 139

    inception of, 46–49

    model, 46, 48

    movement, 46

codependency,

    addiction as family disease and,
        40–43

coining of the term, 9

compared with a crisis, 111–115

cultural bias of, 61–63

existing model, 17

gender bias of, 59–61

humanistic psychotherapy and,
        32–33

is anti-dependent, 63

origins of, 31–43

personal growth and, 62

problem with, 45–68

reasons for popularity of, 32–43

recognition of early-life trauma
        and, 33–36

relationship between masculinity
        and femininity and, 60

view of caregiving and, 4

views of past trauma, 18

the women's movement and, 37–40

codependent, 4, 5, 6

    belief about the ones who love an
        addict, 13

Codependent No More (Beattie), 39,
        48, 54, 55, 63

commitment, 2

compassion, 2

conflict, 63, 100

connection(s),

    addiction and, 13, 75, 96, 118

    addict's pathway to, 117

    in early childhood, 90

    deeper, 106

    desire to retain, 104

    dynamics learned in childhood, 140

    emotional, 71, 72, 74, 143

empathetic, 9
fear of, 86
genetics and, 141–142
healthy, 81, 90, 91, 94, 95, 96, 128
intimate, 21, 72, 86, 95, 115, 134
lacking, 72
loving, 18
meaningful, 105, 142
meaningful social and familial, 72
most important, 115-116
need for, 69–83, 95
ongoing, 27, 29, 82, 87, 100
online, 142
-oriented individuals, 67
oxytocin and, 70
personal growth over shared, 63
prodependent, 28, 97
relational, 87
safe, 105
safety and, 105
shared, 63
social, 89
stable, 115
containment, 12
connection, 13
crisis,
    interpersonal, 5, 16, 17–18, 21, 54
    relationship, 18, 43
    situational, 16
cultural definition of the healthy man,
    60

**D**
deception, 13
denial, 11

breaking through, 12
dependence,
    genetics and, 141–142
Dependent Personality Disorder
    (DPD), 53–54
depression, 20, 28, 35, 49, 70, 73, 75,
    78, 86, 110, 142, 156
"detach with love," 25, 26, 80, 139–140
detachment, vii, 27, 38, 39, 71, 106,
    120, 121, 150
direction, 12
dissociation, 93
distress, 23, 79, 81, 105, 112, 114
dopamine, 70. See also addictive cycle
"driving someone's addiction," 6, 17
DSM, 49, 50
dysfunctional family, 7

**E**
early-life caregivers, 77
enabling, 1, 4, 5, 22, 25, 28, 41, 56, 124,
    126, 150, 153
enmeshed, 5
EMDR, 51–52
emotional intimacy,
    avoiding, 77
    challenges in developing and
        maintaining, 36
    fear of, 28
emotional numbing, 92, 93
emotional reactivity, 16, 151
emotional regulation, 76, 93
emotional well-being, 70. See also
    addictive cycle; serotonin
    attachment and, 72–76

empathetic connection, 9

empathy, 2, 4, 9–10, 54, 60, 61, 68, 107,
        143, 146, 158

endorphins, 70. See also addictive
        cycle; euphoria

euphoria, 70. See also addictive cycle;
        endorphins

Eurocentric treatment models, 62

excitement, 28, 70. See also addictive
        cycle; adrenaline

eye movement desensitization and
        reprocessing. See EMDR

**G**

genetics, 141–142

grief, 2

**H**

healthy love, 2

hope, 12, 146

humanistic psychotherapy, xiv

hypervigilance, 34, 35, 49, 104

**I**

ICD, 50, 52

In the Realm of Hungry Ghosts (Maté),
        70–71

independence, 80–83

insight, 12

interdependence, xv

interpersonal crisis, 5, 16, 17–18, 21,
        54

isolation,
        addiction and, 85–92
        social, 81
        suffering from, 72

**J**

judgment, 4

**L**

Lean on Me (Solomon), 134

loneliness, 28, 70, 77, 81

love,
        meaningful, 17
        and hurt, 103–104
        prodependent, 129, 146–147
        "too much," 19, 109, 135, 150, 158

**M**

meeting people where they are, 9, 11,
        20, 56, 61–62

**N**

National Institute on Drug Abuse, 88

normative response, 16, 17

**O**

Origin of Species, The, (Darwin), xiii,
        xiv

Out of the Shadows (Carnes), xiv

oxytocin, 70

**P**

parents, importance of, 79–80

pathologizing, 5, 6, 16, 17

personal growth, vii, 38, 62, 63, 155

pleasure, 70, 88, 93. See also addictive
        cycle; dopamine

"pleasure drives addiction" viewpoint,
        88

prodependence,
        abuse and, 105–106
        in action, example of, 67–68
        and addicts and their families, 15,
                146–147

care, focus of, 19–21
and causes of drug abuse, 16
celebration of family and friends of addicts, 17
compared to codependence, 16, 17–19
definition of, 15
implications of, 16
imprinting and, 139–141
importance of, 28–29
language of codependence versus, 21–24
main reasons in favor of, 24–28
model, 15–29, 105
the past and, 24
personal differences and, 141–143
primary hypothesis underlying, 18
primary message of, 12
self-care and, 120
summary of, 144–146
view on those who love an addict, 12, 16
prodependent support and therapy, 108–111

**R**
relationship(s),
crisis, 18, 43
dysfunctional, 55
empathetic, nonjudgmental, 10
mutually supportive, 79
prodependent, 131–146
supportive, 27
well-boundaried, 27
re-creation of emotional dynamics of childhood, 13

relaxation, 93
religious beliefs, 61
responsibility, 17, 26, 33, 53, 65, 105, 106, 107, 108, 115, 122, 124, 127, 133, 137, 138

**S**
safety, 79, 102–103, 104, 105, 106, 107, 122, 125, 149
self,
-actualization, 32, 62, 63, 150, 156
-awareness, 32
-care, ii, 25, 28, 62, 68, 107, 111, 113, 115, 119–120, 145, 157
-criticism, 12
-destructive behavior, 75
-development, 38
-doubt, 24
-esteem, 28, 36, 49, 63, 76, 77, 80
-examination, 12
-exploration, 155
-expression, 33
-hatred, 100
-help, 32, 50, 51
-help books, 50, 115
-image, 79
-imposed exile, 89
-imposed isolation, 86
-improvement, 32
-medication, 70
-nurturance, 120
-pity, 56
-preservation, 106
-realization, 135
-regulation, 70, 91, 93

-reliance, 60, 62
-satisfaction, 80
-soothing, 77, 91, 93, 94, 119
-sufficiency, 77, 80, 82
-tests, 57
-will, 69
-worth, 77
serotonin, 70. See also addictive cycle;
    emotional well-being
sexual addiction, xiv
shame, 5, 16, 36, 46, 52, 56, 65, 77, 93,
    95, 97, 100, 102, 117, 120, 131,
    133
situational crisis, 16
social background, 142–143
social isolation, 81
social support, 28
spirituality, 93, 11
stress, 28, 34, 36, 70, 86, 100, 110, 112,
    156
stressors, 70
structure, 12
Substance Abuse and Mental Health
    Administration, 88
support, 4, 12, 40, 67, 73, 76, 90, 107,
    146
  addicts and, 86
  emotional, 64, 70, 71, 78, 93, 99
  empathetic, 66, 95
  groups, 46, 57, 95, 96, 101, 114, 119
  importance of, 80
  interpersonal, 29
  leaning into the collective for, 62
  legal, 102
  loss of, 53

for loved ones, 118–119
  meaningful, 100
  from others and self-esteem, 49
  peer, 47, 100
  prodependent, 108–111
  shared, 39
  social, 28
  successful models of, 61
  therapeutic, 5
systems theory, 32, 40–43

T

trauma,
  bonds, 12–13
  early-life, 13, 17
  movement, xiv
  past, 18, 20, 23, 52, 97, 114, 144,
      146, 150, 154–156
  re-experiencing, 34
  unresolved early-life, 4, 36, 94, 114
trust, 117
twelve-step,
  community, 94
  groups for loved ones of addicts,
      100–102
  programs, 94
  sponsor (or counselor), 11
  support groups, 96

# About the Author

**Robert Weiss, PhD, LCSW**, CEO of Seeking Integrity LLC, is a digital-age sex, intimacy, and relationship specialist. Dr. Weiss has spent more than twenty-five years developing treatment programs, educating clinicians, writing, and providing direct care to those challenged by digital-age infidelity, sexual compulsivity, and other addictive disorders. A clinical sexologist, psychotherapist, and international educator, he frequently serves as a subject matter expert for multiple media outlets including CNN, HLN, MSNBC, Fox, OWN, *The New York Times, The Los Angeles Times,* and NPR, among others.

In addition to *Prodependence,* Dr. Weiss is the author of several highly regarded books on sex and intimacy disorders including *Out of the Doghouse, Sex Addiction 101,* and *Cruise Control,* among others. His *Psychology Today* blog, "Love and Sex in the Digital Age", has over eight million readers to date. He also podcasts *(Sex, Love, & Addiction 101)* and hosts a free, weekly interactive sex and intimacy webinar via *SexandRelationshipHealing.com.*

A skilled clinical educator, Dr. Weiss has created and overseen more than a dozen high-end addiction and mental health treatment programs in the US and abroad. As CEO of Seeking Integrity LLC, he is actively working to create easily accessed, useful, online and real-world solutions that anyone struggling with sex, intimacy, and relationship concerns can utilize. His current project, *SexandRelationshipHealing.com,* is an extensive online resource for recovery from sex and intimacy disorders.

For more information or to reach Dr. Weiss, please visit his website, RobertWeissMSW.com, or follow him on Twitter (@Rob-WeissMSW), LinkedIn (Robert Weiss LCSW), and Facebook (Rob Weiss MSW).